FRENCH PASTRY 101

⇶ *Learn the Art of Classic Baking with 60 Beginner-Friendly Recipes* ⇇

Betty Hung

Owner of Beaucoup Bakery

PAGE STREET
PUBLISHING CO.

PAGE STREET
PUBLISHING CO.

First published in 2018 by

Page Street Publishing Co.

27 Congress Street, Suite 105

Salem, MA 01970

www.pagestreetpublishing.com

Distributed by Macmillan, sales in Canada by The Canadian Manda Group.

22   21   20   19   18   1   2   3   4   5

ISBN-13: 978-1-62414-651-0

ISBN-10: 1-62414-651-1

Library of Congress Control Number: 2018943548

Cover and book design by Rosie Stewart for Page Street Publishing Co.

Photography by Betty Hung

Printed and bound in China

For the passionate, curious and
adventurous home bakers.

For my family, who would always eat
anything I baked.

For my 10-year-old self, who first found
so much joy in baking.

CONTENTS

INTRODUCTION
PÂTISSERIE FOR BEGINNERS

When I was still a home baker, French pastries fascinated me. How could such humble ingredients turn into something so complex and delicious? Many baking techniques as we know them have French roots—I discovered this when I started my pastry apprenticeship. As I immersed myself into the world of pâtisserie, I learned that French pastries are not just about the techniques and ingredients; they are also about precision, temperature, time and the smallest details that make the biggest difference. All of the ingredients in these recipes are provided in volume and weight in grams. I find that measuring in grams yields the most accurate and consistent results. I recommend using a scale to measure all your ingredients, if possible. Making French pastries may seem intimidating to the average home baker. I have baked all the recipes in this book in my home using as few special ingredients and equipment as possible while achieving delicious results. I hope to share some tips and tricks to help any home baker become more confident in their baking projects. Most recipes in this book are meant for beginners, and when you build up your confidence, you can even try to tackle the few advanced recipes!

BASICS

These are some of the fundamental recipes for French pastries. For starters, learning these will lay the foundation for some of the more difficult recipes. One recipe I often revisit is Pâte Sucrée (page 15), which I use for most of my tarts. The Almond Frangipane (page 19) is a versatile filling that is used to fill a variety of pastries such as tarts and even croissants. Crème Pâtissière (page 11) is indispensible when it comes to French pastries; it's used to fill anything from choux puffs to a mille-feuille.

The Creaming Method for Making Pâte Sucrée and Sablés

To have a good foundation for any pastry, you need to learn the basic techniques for making butter-based doughs using the creaming method. A good example is the Pâte Sucrée (page 15) in this chapter and the Spiced Pecan Sablés (page 26) in the Cookies chapter.

To start, make sure your butter is at a good temperature. Cold butter will result in hard chunks in the dough that will melt out as it bakes. If the butter is too soft (as soft as mayonnaise), you'll incorporate too much air in the dough, and it may crumble when you roll it out. The butter is at the perfect temperature when it is soft yet pliable; if you pressed it down with your finger, it should leave a clean dent yet shouldn't stick to your finger.

When creaming the butter and sugar, use the paddle attachment if you are using a stand mixer. Cream it for about 2 minutes at low speed just until the sugar and butter are well incorporated. The key here is not incorporating too much air as mentioned above. When beating in the egg, make sure it is well combined and that the side of the bowl is scraped to ensure all the ingredients are well distributed. After adding the flour, avoid over-mixing the dough. You want to mix it just until there is no more dryness. You can finish mixing by kneading the dough 2 to 3 times with your hands on the counter. Over-mixing will make the gluten bonds stronger, therefore the final product will shrink more and become tough.

It is generally recommended that this type of dough rest in the fridge for 2 to 3 hours or overnight before proceeding. The gluten bonds will relax and the dough becomes easier to roll out and more tender. The sugar will also fully dissolve and result in a more even color after baking.

Whisk the yolks, sugar, salt and cornstarch together.

Temper the egg yolks by slowly incorporating the hot milk.

Return the mixture to the pot to finish cooking.

Whisk the butter into the cooked custard.

Strain the custard to remove any impurities.

Place a piece of plastic wrap directly onto the surface of the custard.

CRÈME PÂTISSIÈRE

This vanilla pastry cream is a versatile filling used in many French pastries such as tarts, éclairs, mille-feuille and more. This recipe is thickened with cornstarch, though some use flour. You can easily infuse other flavors when warming the milk by adding tea leaves and spices. I love using strong teas like English Breakfast or Earl Grey because they give the pastry cream a rich flavor. You can make a spiced pastry cream by infusing a cinnamon stick and a few cardamom pods while warming the milk. This is used in many recipes, such as Coffee Éclairs (page 66), Paris-Brest (page 72) and Mille-Feuille (page 107).

1¼ cups (300 g) whole milk

2 tbsp + 1½ tbsp (52 g) granulated sugar, divided

½ vanilla bean, split and seeds scraped

4 egg yolks

3 tbsp (25 g) cornstarch

A pinch of salt

2 tbsp (30 g) unsalted butter, softened

In a small saucepan, heat the milk on medium heat with 2 tablespoons (30 g) of sugar and the vanilla bean and its seeds until it starts to simmer, about 3 minutes. Turn off the heat, cover the pot and let it steep while you prepare the egg portion of the recipe.

In a medium bowl, whisk together the egg yolks, the remaining sugar, cornstarch and salt. Slowly pour in the hot milk while whisking the egg mixture. Return the mixture to the pot, and turn the heat back on to medium-low. Keep whisking the mixture to keep it from burning on the bottom of the pot, for about 3 to 4 minutes. The pastry cream will start to thicken, and when it starts to boil, it is ready.

Take the pot off the heat, whisk in the butter and strain the cream into a clean bowl. It will be thick, so use a spatula to push it through the strainer. This is to remove the vanilla pod and any impurities such as egg shells. Place a piece of plastic wrap directly onto the surface of the pastry cream to prevent a skin from forming, cool it and store it in the fridge. This can be made up to 3 days in advance.

Tip: This recipe makes a relatively small amount, so it cooks very quickly. Keep whisking the pastry cream as you are cooking to avoid burning it.

CRÈME CHANTILLY

Crème Chantilly may sound fancy, but it is simply whipped cream. However, we often neglect it and over-whip it so it's not enjoyed at its perfect texture. For small batches like this, I like to whip it by hand because there is less chance of over-whipping. Be sure to use a heavy cream or whipping cream. This is used in many recipes such as Frangipane Pear Tart (page 87), Chocolate Torte (page 118) and Praliné Brioche Bread Pudding (page 164).

1 cup (250 g) heavy cream or whipping cream

2 tbsp (30 g) granulated sugar

¼ vanilla bean, seeds scraped or 1 tsp vanilla extract

Place all the ingredients in a medium chilled bowl, and beat vigorously for about 4 minutes—it should start to thicken and form soft peaks. When you lift up your whisk, the tip of the cream should fall over a little, forming a soft peak.

Whipped cream is best enjoyed at this stage. It is also perfect to fold into mousses because it has the right texture. At firm-peak stage, it is stable enough to be piped into different shapes. If you beat it any further, the fat will start to separate from the moisture and you will eventually get butter and a watery milk.

> *Tip:* Whipped cream has a short shelf life and will deflate rather quickly. A great way to stabilize whipped cream is to add skimmed milk powder. Simply add 2 teaspoons (3 g) of milk powder to the above recipe before you whip it.

Combine the ingredients in a chilled bowl.

Whisk the cream vigorously for about 4 minutes.

After about 2 to 3 minutes of whisking, the cream will start to thicken.

The cream is at soft-peak stage when the tip falls over slightly when you lift up your whisk.

Measure and lay out the ingredients.

Add the egg after you have thoroughly creamed the butter and sugar.

Scrape down the sides of the bowl.

Add the flour to the creamed butter, sugar and egg.

Mix the dough until there is no more dry flour.

Form the dough into a disk.

PÂTE SUCRÉE

Pâte sucrée is a cookie-like base that can be used for many sweet tarts. It translates to "sweet paste" in English. This recipe is made using the creaming method. The key is to avoid incorporating too much air into the dough. Pâte sucrée is often formed in the tart pan and blind-baked before adding prepared fillings. This recipe is used in Chocolate Ganache Tart (page 80), Tarte au Citron (page 83), Frangipane Pear Tart (page 87) and Fresh Fig and Orange Tarts (page 88).

1 cup (120 g) powdered sugar

½ tsp salt

¾ cup (170 g) unsalted butter, room temperature

1 large egg, room temperature

1 tsp vanilla extract

2½ cups (350 g) all-purpose flour

Sift together the powdered sugar and salt into a medium bowl. In the bowl of a stand mixer with a paddle attachment, cream the butter on low speed with the sifted powdered sugar for about 2 minutes, until the butter is pale.

Add in the egg and vanilla extract, beat it on medium speed for 2 minutes and scrape down the sides of the bowl. It will look separated, but it will come together once you add the flour. When creaming the butter with the sugar and eggs, avoid incorporating too much air or the dough will crumble easily when you roll it out. The goal is to make a flexible and pliable dough to form into your tart pans.

Mix in the flour at low speed for 30 seconds, or until there is no more dry flour and a dough starts to form. Avoid over-mixing the dough, otherwise it will shrink when baked and yield a tough pastry.

Transfer the dough onto a clean work surface, gather and form it into a disk, wrap it in plastic and let it chill in the fridge for at least 30 minutes to firm up. You can also make this up to 3 days in advance.

Tip: The dough scraps can be either re-rolled into more tarts or made into cookies.

PÂTE BRISÉE

Pâte brisée is a tender shortcrust dough that is typically used in tarts. It yields a buttery and sturdy yet flaky crust for pastries such as fruit tarts and quiches. This recipe also works beautifully as crusts for your favorite pies. In this book, it is used for the Flan Pâtissier (page 49), Tarte aux Pommes (page 84) and Quiche Lorraine (page 91). The pâte brisée can be made in a mixer, food processor or by hand. The following method is by hand; it's very easy to do and you have less chance of over-mixing the dough.

1¾ cups (245 g) all-purpose flour

1 tbsp (15 g) granulated sugar

1 tsp salt

1 large egg, cold

3 tbsp (45 g) whole milk, cold

1 cup (227 g) cold unsalted butter, cut into small cubes

In a medium mixing bowl, whisk together the flour, sugar and salt. In a separate bowl, whisk together the egg and milk.

Place the cold butter into the flour mixture. Using a pastry blender or your hands, quickly cut the butter into small chunks.

Pour in the wet ingredients. Blend the ingredients with a scraper or your hands to form coarse chunks. Transfer it to a clean work surface and knead the dough with your hands by pushing the dough and folding it. Repeat this process about 10 times, until you have a cohesive dough. Avoid over-kneading, otherwise it will shrink when baked and yield a tough pastry. Streaks of butter in the dough is what you are looking for; this is what makes the pastry flaky and tender. If you can't see the butter streaks, you may have over-mixed it.

Form the dough into a round disk, wrap it in plastic wrap and refrigerate it for at least 30 minutes, or preferably overnight, before using it.

Make sure you use cold butter in this recipe.

Cut the butter into small chunks with a pastry blender.

The butter should be in uniform, pea-sized chunks.

Add the cold egg and milk mixture to incorporate the ingredients and form coarse chunks.

Knead the dough until it comes together. You should see butter streaks throughout the dough.

Shape it into a round disk before wrapping and chilling.

Measure and lay out your ingredients.

Cream the butter and dry ingredients.

Add the egg and mix until the frangipane is fluffy.

The finished frangipane should be cohesive and well mixed.

ALMOND FRANGIPANE

⇒ *Prep Time: 15 minutes - Makes 1¾ cups (360 g)* ⇐

Almond frangipane is a very versatile filling. It is used in tarts, croissants and pastries. It has a texture between cake, marzipan and custard. With its wonderful almond flavor, it makes a great companion to apples, pears, stone fruits and berries. Have all the ingredients at room temperature and you will have no problem making this delicious filling. This recipe is used in Frangipane Pear Tart (page 87), Galette des Rois (page 103) and Almond Croissants (page 159).

1 cup (100 g) almond flour, preferably very fine

¾ cup + 2 tbsp (100 g) powdered sugar

1 tbsp (10 g) cornstarch

½ tsp salt

7 tbsp (100 g) unsalted butter, room temperature

1 large egg, room temperature

1 tsp vanilla extract

Sift the almond flour, powdered sugar, cornstarch and salt into a medium bowl.

In a large mixing bowl, beat the butter with a rubber spatula until soft, then add in the sifted almond flour and sugar mixture. Continue mixing the ingredients by hand until everything is incorporated. Add in the egg and vanilla extract and mix until the frangipane is fluffy.

Transfer the finished frangipane to a clean container or directly into a piping bag, and store it in the fridge until ready to use. You can make this up to 3 days in advance.

Tip: You can replace the almond flour with other nut flours such as hazelnuts or use a combination of different nuts.

HAZELNUT PRALINÉ

⇒ *Prep Time: 45 minutes - Makes 1 cup (250 g)* ⇐

Praliné is the base for many French pastry fillings, most notably Paris-Brest. It is a paste made by grinding caramelized nuts, and this recipe uses hazelnuts. It could also be used in chocolate ganache, or as a bonbon filling. You may be able to find praliné in specialty food stores, but professional pastry kitchens often get it from their suppliers. I think it is worth making at home, and once you taste it, you'll understand why. This recipe is used in Paris-Brest (page 72) and Praliné Brioche Bread Pudding (page 164).

1½ cups (200 g) skinned hazelnuts

½ cup + 2 tbsp (140 g) sugar

2 tbsp (30 g) water

½ tsp salt

¼ vanilla bean, seeds scraped

If you can't find skinned hazelnuts, roast hazelnuts in a 325°F (160°C) oven for about 10 minutes, until the skin can be easily rubbed off. While the nuts are warm, rub off the skin with a clean, dry tea towel or with your fingers. Don't worry about getting all the skin off, as long as most of the nuts are skinned.

Line a baking sheet with parchment paper, and set it aside.

In a medium saucepan, combine the sugar and water. Heat the sugar on medium heat until it boils, for about 3 minutes. Add the nuts and stir to coat them with the syrup. Don't stop mixing the nuts. The sugar will start to crystallize, covering the nuts after about 5 to 7 minutes. This is normal, but it is important to keep stirring the nuts because the sugar will eventually caramelize and you don't want them to burn.

As the sugar caramelizes, keep an eye on it; you want to cook it to a deep amber color, not too dark. When the sugar has reached a deep amber, about 7 to 8 minutes, take the pot off the heat and spread the nuts onto the parchment-lined baking sheet. Make sure you do this quickly as the caramel will harden as it cools. The caramel will be hot, so be careful not to burn yourself.

After cooling, process the nuts with the salt and vanilla seeds in a food processor. It will take about 5 minutes for the nuts to become powdery and then turn into a paste.

Store the paste in a clean, dry jar in the fridge for up to a month.

Tips: This recipe contains about a 60 percent nuts to 40 percent sugar ratio, which is considered high. You can decrease the nuts to a 50/50 ratio, but it will be a sweeter paste. You can also use other nuts such as almonds or walnuts, but nuts vary in their oil content, which will yield different consistencies.

This recipe uses only the vanilla bean seeds, but save the pod and use it to flavor sugar or even salt.

Add the nuts into the syrup and keep stirring as the sugar cooks.

After 5 to 7 minutes, the sugar will start to crystallize, coating the nuts.

After cooking for 7 to 8 more minutes, the sugar will start to caramelize.

When the sugar has turned a deep amber color, quickly transfer the nuts onto a parchment-lined tray.

COOKIES

Sablés are some of the most common cookies found in French bakeries. In fact, in France, the term cookie refers to North American–style cookies. In this chapter, you will start by learning the basic sablé (Spiced Pecan Sablés, page 26), and then how to turn them into different variations. Vanilla Madeleines (page 37) and Financiers (page 38) are some of my favorite French pastries to make; they are so simple and delicious. If you are ready for a challenge, try the Florentines (page 43); their complexity is well worth the time.

Most cookies in this chapter bake at a lower temperature for a longer time. This is to bake out all the moisture so the cookies have a sandy and crisp texture. If the temperature is too high, you risk burning the edges while the center may still be raw.

Piping Batter into Straight Lines

The Ladyfingers (page 34) and Langues de Chat (page 30) recipes in this chapter are great for practicing your piping skills. Don't focus on getting them perfect the first few tries. Once you practice more, this skill can be transferred to many other pastries. Remember to keep your piping tip at a 90-degree angle and at a short distance from the tray. Pipe slowly and gently; let the batter lie onto the sheet instead of pressing the tip onto the tray when you pipe. That way you will get straight and consistent lines. If you are after a specific measurement or shape, mark the dimensions on a piece of parchment paper. Prior to making your batter, flip the paper over to line your tray and use the markings as a guide when piping. Aim to pipe a consistent size because larger cookies will take longer to cook while smaller ones will cook faster.

SABLÉ BRETON

Sablé Breton originated in the Brittany region of France, an area known for its delicious butter and salt. *Sablé* means "sandy" while *Breton* means Brittany. A shiny top with a crisscross pattern is the signature of these French butter cookies. Their rich buttery flavor and sandy texture are simply irresistible, perfect with a cup of hot coffee. Try using a high-fat or "European style" butter for this recipe; the cookies will be even more buttery and tender. This can also be used as a base for tarts (page 79).

2 egg yolks, room temperature

½ vanilla pod, seeds scraped or 1 tsp vanilla extract

½ cup + 2 tbsp (125 g) granulated sugar

1 cup + 2 tbsp (160 g) all-purpose flour

1¾ tsp (6 g) baking powder

1 tsp salt

½ cup (113 g) unsalted butter, room temperature (if using salted butter, reduce added salt by ½ tsp)

Egg wash (1 egg yolk whisked with 1 tbsp [15 g] of water and a pinch of salt)

In the bowl of a stand mixer with the paddle attachment, beat the egg yolks, vanilla seeds or extract and sugar on medium speed for about a minute. Meanwhile, sift together the flour, baking powder and salt into a medium bowl.

Stop the mixer, add the butter and mix on medium speed for 30 seconds, until the mixture comes together.

Scrape down the sides of the bowl with a spatula, and add the sifted flour mixture. Mix on low speed for about 30 seconds, until there are no more dry flour bits. Avoid over-mixing, which will make the cookies turn out hard and tough.

Transfer the dough onto a work surface, gather and pat it into a disk (about 6 inches [15 cm] across). Wrap the dough in plastic and chill it in the refrigerator for 30 minutes before rolling. You can prepare the dough up to 3 days in advance and store it in the fridge; let the dough sit out at room temperature for 20 minutes to soften before rolling.

Preheat the oven to 350°F (180°C), and line two baking sheets with parchment paper.

To roll and cut the cookies, lightly dust the work surface with flour, just enough so the dough won't stick to your rolling pin. Gently roll out the slab, turning it 90 degrees after each roll, until it's about ¼ inch (6 mm) thick.

Cut with a 2½-inch (6-cm) round cutter. Gather any scraps to re-roll and cut out more cookies.

Place the cookies on the parchment-lined baking sheets about 1 inch (2.5 cm) apart. Lightly brush the tops of the cookies with the egg wash. Score a crosshatch pattern with a fork on each cookie. Bake, one tray at a time, for 15 to 18 minutes, rotating the baking sheet halfway through, until the edges are golden brown. Cool the cookies completely before serving, and store them in an airtight container for up to a week.

Tip: Roll the cookies to a consistent thickness so they will bake and brown evenly. If the dough becomes too soft, chill it briefly in the fridge to firm it up before rolling again.

SPICED PECAN SABLÉS

This recipe is a twist on the more typical almond sablés. I have used pecans in the place of almonds and added spices, which makes this a great holiday cookie. Walnuts also work beautifully in this recipe. You can usually substitute nuts by weight in a simple recipe like this; however, keep in mind that different nuts have different fat contents. For example, walnuts and pecans are oilier than almonds and hazelnuts, so the nut you choose may affect the final result.

1½ cups (210 g) all-purpose flour

¾ cup (90 g) pecans, toasted and finely crushed, reserve 2 tbsp (15 g) for the topping

¾ tsp ground cinnamon

¼ tsp ground nutmeg

1 tsp salt

⅔ cup (150 g) unsalted butter, room temperature

½ cup + 2 tsp (110 g) granulated sugar

2 tbsp (30 g) whole egg, room temperature

1 tsp vanilla extract

1 tsp bourbon (optional)

Egg wash (1 egg yolk whisked with 1 tbsp [15 g] of water and a pinch of salt)

In a medium bowl, whisk together the flour, pecans, cinnamon, nutmeg and salt. Set it aside until ready to use.

In the bowl of a stand mixer with the paddle attachment, combine the butter and sugar, beating on medium speed until the mixture becomes pale, about 3 minutes. Add the egg, vanilla and bourbon, and mix on medium speed for another 3 minutes, until the mixture is incorporated.

Stop mixing, and scrape down the sides of the bowl with a spatula. Add the dry ingredients, and start the mixer on low. Mix for about 30 seconds, just until there is no more dryness in the dough. If necessary, scrape down the sides of the bowl and mix on low for 10 more seconds.

Take the dough from the bowl, and shape it into a square roughly 6 inches (15 cm) across. Wrap it with plastic wrap and let it rest in the fridge for at least an hour or overnight.

When you are ready to roll out the dough, preheat the oven to 325°F (160°C). Line two baking sheets with parchment paper.

Divide the dough into two pieces for easier rolling. Lightly dust your dough and work surface with flour. Start rolling the dough from the center to the edge, rotating the dough 90 degrees after each roll and dusting with flour if necessary. Roll the dough to about ¼ inch (6 mm) thick. Cut out 2 x 2¾–inch (5 x 7–cm) diamond shapes, and place them about 1 inch (2.5 cm) apart on the baking sheets. If you don't have a diamond cutter, use a 2-inch (5-cm) round cutter.

Lightly brush a layer of egg wash on the cookies, avoiding the edges, and sprinkle the reserved pecans on top.

Bake the cookies for 20 to 25 minutes, rotating the baking sheets halfway through, until the edges and bottoms are golden brown. Cool the cookies before serving. Store them in an airtight container for up to a week.

PISTACHIO RASPBERRY SANDWICH COOKIES

⇒ *Prep Time: 45 minutes - Makes 28 sandwich cookies* ⇐

This recipe is my twist on Linzer cookies, which are commonly made with almonds or hazelnuts. I love the delectable combination of pistachios and raspberries. By elaborating the basic sablé recipe (Spiced Pecan Sablés, page 26) with some small changes, these have turned into completely different cookies.

1½ cups (225 g) all-purpose flour

½ cup (65 g) shelled pistachios, lightly roasted and finely crushed

1 tsp salt

⅔ cup (150 g) unsalted butter, room temperature

½ cup + 2 tsp (110 g) granulated sugar

2 tsp (10 g) vanilla extract

2 tbsp (30 g) whole egg, room temperature

1 cup (250 g) raspberry jam

2 tbsp (13 g) powdered sugar, for garnish

In a medium bowl, whisk together the flour, pistachios and salt. Set it aside until ready to use.

In the bowl of a stand mixer, using the paddle attachment, combine the butter and granulated sugar, and beat on medium speed until it becomes pale, about 3 minutes. Add the vanilla and egg, and mix on medium speed for another 3 minutes, until the mixture is incorporated. Stop mixing and scrape down the sides of the bowl with a spatula.

Add the dry ingredients, and start the mixer on low. Mix for about 30 seconds, just until there is no more dry flour in the dough. If necessary, scrape down the sides of the bowl and mix on low for 10 more seconds.

Take the dough from the bowl, and shape it into a roughly 6-inch (15-cm) square. Wrap it with plastic wrap and let it rest in the fridge for at least an hour or overnight.

When you are ready to roll your dough, preheat the oven to 325°F (160°C). Line two baking sheets with parchment paper.

Divide your dough into two for easier rolling. Lightly dust the dough and work surface with flour. Start rolling the dough from the center to the edge, rotating 90 degrees after each roll, dusting on a little flour if necessary. Roll the dough to about ⅛ inch (3 mm) thick.

Cut into 2-inch (5-cm) fluted rounds. Place the cookies about 1 inch (2.5 cm) apart on the first baking sheet. Repeat the rolling and cutting with the other half of the dough, with smaller cutters, and cut out the desired shapes. Arrange the cookies in the same manner on the second baking sheet as the solid cookies.

Bake the cookies with the cut-outs for 10 to 15 minutes, and the ones without for 15 to 20 minutes, rotating the baking sheets halfway through, until the edges and bottoms are golden brown.

To fill, turn the solid cookies flat-side up, and spoon about ½ teaspoon of jam onto each cookie. Dust the top of the cut-out cookies with powdered sugar, and sandwich them, pressing the flat sides together. The cookies are best served right after filling.

LANGUES DE CHAT

Langue de chat means "cat's tongue" in English, which are what these cookies resemble. This is a relatively simple recipe; the trick is to get the butter very soft so the ingredients can emulsify properly. These cookies are a great treat with a cup of hot coffee or tea. Though some recipes don't add almond flour, I find that it gives the cookies a wonderful flavor and tender texture.

7 tbsp (100 g) unsalted butter, very soft (like mayonnaise)

¾ cup + 1 tbsp (81 g) powdered sugar, sifted

½ cup (45 g) almond flour

½ tsp vanilla extract

3 large egg whites (between ⅓ cup + 1 tbsp to ¾ cup [100 g]), room temperature

⅓ cup + 3 tbsp (48 g) cake flour, sifted

½ tsp salt

Preheat the oven to 325°F (160°C). Line two baking sheets with parchment paper.

In the bowl of a mixer with a paddle attachment, combine the butter and powdered sugar at medium speed for 3 minutes, until the mixture is light and fluffy. Add in the almond flour, and continue mixing on medium speed for another 3 minutes.

Scrape down the sides of the bowl, add the vanilla extract, then the egg whites in three additions, mixing on medium speed for 30 seconds after each addition, until well combined. The mixture will look grainy, but it will come together when you add the cake flour.

Take the bowl off the mixer, and fold in the cake flour and salt with a spatula. You should mix until it's just combined; the batter will be a thick paste.

Prepare a piping bag with a 1-centimeter round tip. Pipe the batter into 2-inch (5-cm) lines, spacing the cookies at least an inch (2.5 cm) from each other. One sheet should fit 21 cookies in three rows of 7. For tips on piping, refer to page 23.

Bake the cookies for 23 to 25 minutes, rotating the baking sheets halfway through, until the edges and bottoms are golden brown. Cool the cookies completely before serving. Store them in an airtight container for up to a week.

Tips: The texture of the butter has to be very soft in this recipe, otherwise it will not emulsify with the egg whites. In French, this is called beurre pomade; when the butter is between 68° to 86°F (20° to 30°C), it should be spreadable, like mayonnaise.

The egg whites should be at room temperature; cold ones will seize the butter and the batter will not emulsify properly.

BROWN BUTTER ALMOND TUILES

⇉ *Prep Time: 30 minutes* - *Makes 24 cookies* ⇐

Almond tuiles are another classic French cookie. These thin, crispy wafers get their signature curved shape when draped over a rolling pin while hot. These make an excellent companion to desserts or coffee. They can even be turned into ice-cream bowls if made bigger and draped over the bottom of a bowl to cool. This tuile recipe has brown butter, which is not traditional but adds a wonderful nutty caramel flavor to the cookies.

3½ tbsp (50 g) unsalted butter

½ cup + 2 tbsp (125 g) granulated sugar

2 tbsp + 2 tsp (40 g) egg whites, room temperature

3 tbsp + 1 tsp (50 g) whole milk

½ tsp vanilla extract

⅓ cup (40 g) cake flour, sifted

½ tsp salt

¾ cup (80 g) sliced blanched almonds

Preheat the oven to 325°F (160°C). Line two baking sheets with silicone mats or parchment paper. Silicone mats yield a smoother bottom and a more even bake.

In a small saucepan, heat the butter over medium heat until it turns brown and fragrant, about 2 to 3 minutes. Set it aside to cool.

In a medium bowl, whisk together the sugar and egg whites until the sugar has dissolved. Add the milk and vanilla extract to incorporate.

Add the flour and the salt and whisk until the batter is smooth. Fold in the sliced almonds with a spatula until they are evenly distributed.

Drop heaping teaspoons of the batter onto the baking sheets, spaced about 2 inches (5 cm) apart. The cookies will expand quite a bit. Bake one tray at a time for 15 to 18 minutes, until the edges turn golden. Take out the cookies and let them cool for 20 seconds. Using a small offset spatula, carefully lift the cookies, and drape them over a clean rolling pin to create their curved shape. If the cookies become too stiff, return them to the oven for about 20 seconds and try again. Cool them completely before serving. Store them in a clean, airtight container for up to 3 days.

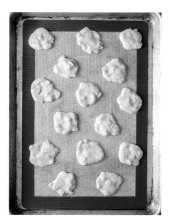

LADYFINGERS

⇒ *Prep Time: 30 minutes - Makes 40 cookies* ⇐

Ladyfingers are made from sponge cake batter piped into short "fingers." They are often used as dessert bases in a charlotte (see page 125) or tiramisu. Because they are a little dry, they hold their shape well, which makes them great for dunking into hot beverages. This recipe uses only four ingredients and is a great way to practice your piping skills (page 23). Also, the batch size is perfect for making in the stand mixer rather than a smaller batch.

¾ cup + 2 tbsp (105 g) all-purpose flour

4 large eggs, room temperature, separated

½ cup + 1 tbsp (120 g) granulated sugar

½ cup (50 g) powdered sugar, for dusting

Preheat the oven to 400°F (200°C). Line three baking trays with parchment paper and set them aside.

Sift the flour into a medium bowl and set it aside.

Whip the egg whites with the whisk attachment in a stand mixer for about 30 seconds at medium speed until they become frothy. Slowly sprinkle in the granulated sugar and whip on high speed for about 3 minutes, until the meringue is fluffy and forms medium peaks. When you lift the whisk, the tip of the meringue should hold its shape, while curling over itself.

Add the egg yolks and mix on medium speed for another 3 minutes, until the batter leaves a trail. As with making all sponges, make sure you whip the eggs and sugar to the "ribbon" stage; when the batter falls on itself, you can see an obvious trail. For tips on making sponge cakes, refer to page 109.

Gently fold in the sifted flour until there is no more visible dry flour. To avoid deflating the batter, don't over-mix.

Fill a piping bag with a 1-centimeter round tip with about half of the batter. Pipe out 4-inch (10-cm)-long lines, spacing about 1 inch (2.5 cm) apart. Dust the tops generously with powdered sugar. Repeat the piping and dusting with the rest of the batter. For tips on piping, refer to page 23.

Bake one tray at a time for 8 to 10 minutes, until the ladyfingers are puffy and slightly golden around the edges. They are best eaten the day they are baked. If you're using them as a base for desserts, you can bake them up to a week ahead.

Tips: The batter will deflate quickly once you fold in the flour; pipe quickly so the batter doesn't flatten out on the tray.

When baking these cookies, 1 to 2 minutes less or more makes a big difference. The ideal texture is a little crisp on the outside and soft inside. When baked too long, they will turn out crunchy.

VANILLA MADELEINES

➤ *Prep Time: 30 minutes - Makes 24 cookies* ⬅

Madeleines are best when they are warm and fresh out of the oven. Their crispy edges and moist, tender crumbs are divine. Madeleines are a cross between a cookie and a cake, and are usually served with hot coffee or tea. For the French, the mark of a perfect madeleine is the bump on the back of its signature fluted shell shape. The key to achieving this shape is resting the batter and baking them at a high temperature for a short period of time.

1⅓ cups (200 g) all-purpose flour

2¼ tsp (8 g) baking powder

½ tsp salt

¾ cup (150 g) granulated sugar

½ vanilla bean, split and seeds scraped

3 large eggs, room temperature

½ cup (113 g) unsalted butter, melted and cooled

⅓ cup + 1 tbsp (75 g) whole milk, room temperature

Powdered sugar, for garnish (optional)

In a medium bowl, whisk together the flour, baking powder and salt.

In a separate bowl, measure the sugar and mix in the vanilla seeds with your fingers to evenly distribute them.

In a large mixing bowl, beat the eggs and sugar vigorously until it becomes frothy, about 2 to 3 minutes. Fold in the dry ingredients with a spatula until the flour is just incorporated. Add in the melted butter and milk, and fold until they're incorporated. Cover and rest the batter in the fridge for at least 2 hours, preferably overnight.

When you're ready to bake, preheat the oven to 500°F (250°C). Generously butter the wells of the madeleine pans, dust with flour and tap out the extra. Fill a piping bag with batter and pipe it into the pan. If you prefer, you can also spoon the batter into the molds. Once filled, lightly tap the pan on the counter to level the batter and remove any large air pockets.

Bake them for 3 minutes, then lower the temperature to 425°F (220°C) and bake for 7 to 8 minutes more. Be careful not to over-bake them; the edges should be golden and the tops should spring back when you press them with your finger.

While still warm, turn the madeleines out onto a cooling rack. Dust with powdered sugar, if desired. Serve warm; they are best served the day they are baked.

Tip: To melt the butter, place it in a heatproof bowl set over simmering water. This is the easiest way to melt butter without having to worry about it boiling over or burning. You can also use a microwave. Place the butter in a microwave-safe bowl and heat for 30 to 40 seconds on high. Keep an eye on it, because it may boil over and spatter. For this recipe, you want to use the butter while it is still in its liquid state, but not hot.

FINANCIERS

The name *financier* is said to have come from the appearance of these almond cakes resembling gold bars. What makes them so special is the beurre noisette, or brown butter, which gives them a nutty, caramel flavor. This recipe is very easy to put together; the trick is to brown the butter until it is deeply golden and aromatic. The best part of these cookies is the contrast between their crispy edges and soft center.

¾ cup (170 g) unsalted butter

¾ cup (60 g) almond flour

⅓ cup + 1 tbsp (60 g) cake flour, sifted

1 tsp salt

5 large egg whites (⅔ cup [156 g]), room temperature

¾ cup + 1 tbsp (156 g) granulated sugar

1 tsp vanilla extract or the seeds from ½ vanilla bean

2 tbsp (50 g) honey (For this recipe, I used a dark honey that stands up to the nutty brown butter.)

To make the brown butter, place the butter in a saucepan over medium heat and swirl the pan every minute or so; the butter will foam and separate. The key is to cook it until it becomes deep brown; it will be very aromatic. This process should take 8 to 9 minutes. Keep an eye on it; the butter can burn easily. Set the butter aside while you prepare the rest of the recipe. You should use the brown butter while it is in its liquid state or lukewarm. Some recipes suggest straining out the brown milk solids after you brown your butter, but I find the brown bits give these cakes a deeper flavor. If you wish, you can strain out the bits before adding it to your batter.

In a medium bowl, combine the almond flour, cake flour and salt. In another bowl, whisk together the egg whites, sugar and vanilla extract or seeds until frothy, about 1 to 2 minutes. Whisk in the flour mixture, mixing only until the batter comes together.

Add in the liquid brown butter and honey and fold them in with a spatula. Transfer the batter into a container, cover and chill it for at least 2 hours or overnight.

When you are ready to fill the molds, preheat the oven to 450°F (230°C). Grease the financier tins generously with softened butter, dust with flour and tap out the extra. Fill the tins with the batter until they're level; you can use an offset spatula to level off the tins. If you don't have rectangular molds, a mini muffin pan works just as well. Grease and fill the cups the same way and decrease the bake time by 1 to 2 minutes.

Place the filled tins on a baking sheet. Bake the financiers for 10 to 15 minutes, rotating the baking sheet halfway through, until the edges are a deep golden brown. While the financiers are slightly warm, carefully unmold them and cool them on a rack. They are best eaten the day they are baked.

Tips: When greasing any baking pans or molds, always use softened butter (the consistency of mayonnaise). That way you can brush on a thick layer of butter that will stay on the pan's surface unlike liquid butter that will settle in the bottom. This method will make the baked good release easier, and contribute to a more even browning during baking.

Make sure you bake the financiers until they are a deep brown around the edges—they will release easier from the tins and have a crispy, chewy exterior.

   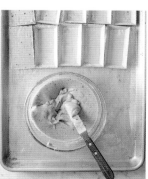

RASPBERRY HAZELNUT FINANCIERS

⇒ *Prep Time: 40 minutes* - *Makes ten 4¼ x 2–inch (11 x 5–cm) boat-shaped cakes* ⇐

Fresh fruit is not a typical ingredient in financiers, but I love the raspberries and orange zest here because it makes these cakes taste so refreshing. Instead of using almonds, I have used toasted hazelnuts, which have a much bolder flavor. This recipe is an easy way to dress up the classic.

½ cup (113 g) unsalted butter

⅓ cup (50 g) whole hazelnuts, plus more for garnish

⅓ cup (50 g) cake flour, sifted

½ tsp salt

4 large egg whites (½ cup [125 g]), room temperature

½ cup + 2 tbsp (125 g) granulated sugar

1 tsp vanilla extract

1 tbsp (25 g) dark honey

2 tsp (4 g) orange zest, finely grated

2 tsp (10 g) hazelnut liqueur (optional)

1 cup (100 g) fresh raspberries

2 tbsp (13 g) powdered sugar, for garnish

To make the brown butter, place the butter in a saucepan over medium heat and swirl the pan every minute or so; the butter will foam and separate. The key is to cook it until it becomes deep brown; it will be very aromatic. This process should take 8 to 9 minutes. Keep an eye on it; the butter can burn easily. Set the butter aside while you prepare the rest of the recipe. You should use the brown butter while it is in its liquid state or lukewarm. Some recipes suggest straining out the brown milk solids after you brown your butter, but I find the brown bits give these cakes a deeper flavor. If you wish, you can strain out the bits before adding it to your batter.

To roast the hazelnuts, preheat the oven to 325°F (160°C). Spread the hazelnuts on a baking sheet, and roast them for 15 minutes until golden and aromatic. If your hazelnuts are not blanched, remove their skins while they are still hot by rubbing them with a clean kitchen towel. Cool the nuts and finely crush or grind them. You can use a food processor. Make sure you don't grind the nuts too much, otherwise they will start to form a nut butter.

In a medium bowl, combine the ground hazelnuts, cake flour and salt.

In another bowl, whisk the egg whites, granulated sugar and vanilla extract until frothy, about 1 to 2 minutes. Whisk in the flour mixture, mixing only until the batter comes together.

Using a spatula, fold in the liquid brown butter, honey, orange zest and liqueur. Transfer the batter into a container, cover and refrigerate for at least 2 hours or overnight.

When you are ready to fill the molds, preheat the oven to 450°F (230°C). Grease the financier tins generously with softened butter, dust with flour and tap out any extra. Using a spoon or piping bag, fill the tins with the batter until almost full (about 90 percent).

(continued)

Place the filled tins on a baking sheet. Top each financier with three fresh raspberries and crushed hazelnuts, if you wish. If you don't have boat-shaped molds, a mini muffin pan works just as well. Grease and fill the cups the same way, top with two raspberries and decrease the bake time between 1 and 3 minutes.

Bake the financiers for 15 to 18 minutes, rotating the baking sheet halfway through, until the edges are a deep golden brown. Cool the financiers to room temperature, and unmold them onto a rack. Lightly dust the tops with powdered sugar before serving. They are best eaten the day they are baked.

Tips: If you can find hazelnut flour, replace the whole hazelnuts with ½ cup + 2 teaspoons (63 g) of hazelnut flour. It will save you from skinning and grinding whole nuts; all you need to do is toast it until fragrant. However, I find that whole hazelnuts are much more flavorful than the flour.

Other nuts such as almonds and pistachios work well in this recipe. If you use almond flour, use ½ cup + 2 teaspoons (50 g). If using pistachios, use the same measurements as the hazelnuts in the recipe.

FLORENTINES

I have fond memories of my first Florentine cookie. At first, I was skeptical at its appearance, but as I tasted it, I was so surprised at how complex it was. The cookie base was buttery and tender, and the top was a soft, chewy caramel with nuts and candied orange peel. Not to be confused with Florentine lace cookies, this recipe is made of a shortbread-type base topped with honey caramel and almonds, sliced into bars or squares. The base is a simple cookie dough, but the caramel requires a little more attention; the trick is cooking it to the right temperature and baking it to the perfect color. This is an advanced cookie recipe that requires making two components, but with a little patience you should be well on your way.

Base

⅔ cup (150 g) unsalted butter, room temperature

⅓ cup (75 g) granulated sugar

2 tbsp (30 g) whole egg, room temperature

½ tsp salt

1⅓ cups (200 g) all-purpose flour

In a mixer with the paddle attachment, combine the butter and sugar, beating on medium speed until it becomes pale, about 3 minutes. Add the egg, and mix on medium speed for another 3 minutes, until the mixture is incorporated. Stop mixing and scrape down the sides of the bowl with a spatula.

Add the salt and flour, and start the mixer on low. Mix for about 30 seconds, just until there is no more dry flour in the dough. If necessary, scrape down the sides of the bowl and mix on low for 10 more seconds.

Take the dough from the bowl, and shape it into a square of roughly 6 inches (15 cm). Wrap it with plastic wrap and let it rest in the fridge for at least an hour or overnight.

When you are ready to roll your dough, preheat the oven to 350°F (180°C). Line the bottom of a 9 x 13–inch (23 x 33–cm) pan with parchment paper.

Lightly dust your dough and work surface with flour. Start rolling the dough from the center to the edge. Rotate the dough 90 degrees after each roll, and dust with a little flour if necessary. Roll the dough to 9 x 13 inches (23 x 33 cm).

To transfer the dough sheet, roll it around your rolling pin, line up the end of the sheet to the end of your pan and unroll it onto the bottom of the pan. Using your fingers, gently press the dough into the corners of the pan. Using a paring knife, trim the dough about ¼ inch (6 mm) along the top edge. Pressing and trimming the dough will create edges that contain the caramel in the crust as it cooks, and the cookies will not stick to the edge of the pan.

Dock the bottom with a fork (see page 94), and bake for 15 minutes, rotating the pan halfway through, until the edges are slightly golden. Take it out and let it cool while you make the caramel.

(continued)

Honey-Almond Caramel

⅓ cup + 1 tbsp (80 g) granulated sugar

1 tbsp + 2 tsp (36 g) honey

¼ cup (60 g) whipping cream

1 tbsp (15 g) unsalted butter

½ cup (60 g) blanched sliced almonds

½ tsp salt

1 tsp vanilla extract

1 tbsp (15 g) candied orange peel, finely chopped

In a medium saucepan, combine all the ingredients except for the vanilla extract and orange peel, and cook over medium heat. For tips on making the perfect caramel, see page 48. Cook the caramel until it starts to bubble on the surface, to about 230°F (110°C), and stir in the vanilla extract and candied orange peel. Pour the caramel almond mixture onto the baked crust, and carefully spread it evenly.

Bake the cookies at 350°F (180°C) for 10 to 12 minutes. The caramel will be lightly golden and the surface will be bubbly. Use caution when you take the pan out of the oven, and let it cool completely before cutting it. It is important not to over-bake these because you want the caramel to stay soft and chewy, which is what makes these cookies so special and delicious.

To cut the cookies, carefully flip them onto a cutting board so the caramel side is on the bottom. Using a serrated knife, cut off 1 centimeter along one short and long edge. Using a ruler and knife, mark the size of the cookies to approximately 1 x 1½ inches (2.5 x 4 cm). Cut the cookies in a gentle sawing motion. Flip them over to serve. They will keep up to a week in an airtight container, or you can freeze them up to a month.

Tips: The caramel is traditionally made with chestnut honey, which has a strong taste and might be difficult to source in North America. I have used a light honey, but you can substitute a dark honey if you prefer a bolder flavor.

The candied orange peels bring together all the flavors and textures of these Florentine cookies, so use a good-quality product if you can.

CUSTARDS

Custards are made with eggs, sugar and milk. Different ratios determine the different varieties. Many French pastries use custard fillings, such as pastry cream. Classic custard desserts such as Earl Grey Crème Caramel (page 55) and Crème Brûlée (page 56) are some of the basic must-learn French desserts. One of the skills to tackle when making custards is tempering the eggs with hot milk to emulsify the hot milk and eggs. The key is to keep whisking the eggs while you slowly pour in the hot milk. If you add the hot milk all at once to the eggs, the eggs start to cook and solidify, which you want to avoid.

Many French dessert recipes, such as the crème caramel recipe in this chapter (page 55), require cooking caramel. Making caramel is merely cooking sugar to a high enough temperature so it caramelizes just before it burns.

To start, make sure there are no impurities in the sugar and your pot is clean and dry. Sugar tends to crystallize on foreign particles as it cooks, so having a clean pot and pure granulated sugar helps avoid this. A little bit of acidity also prevents crystallization; that is why some recipes will include a small amount of lemon juice or cream of tartar.

Generally speaking, you want to cook the caramel in as little time as possible, so it has the least chance of crystallizing. However, you may burn the sugar quickly on high heat depending on the amount in your recipe. So, I usually start at medium-high heat. The time really depends on the amount of sugar you are cooking, so invest in a candy thermometer if you are serious about candy making. If you are just cooking the caramel, as for the crème caramel recipe, you can use smell and sight to determine its readiness.

When cooking sugar with water, it will go through different stages: hard ball (250°–256°F [122°–125°C]), soft crack (270°–290°F [132°–143°C]), hard crack (300°–310°F [150°–155°C]) and caramel (320°F [160°C]). Before the caramel stage, the sugar in the syrup will continue to cook down; at this point you have to be careful of crystals forming. You also want to avoid stirring it for this reason. Instead, swirl the pot once every 1 to 2 minutes as the syrup cooks, and if you see sugar forming on the walls of the pot, brush a little water around the inside of the pot where the crystals are forming. When the syrup starts to turn yellow (320°F [160°C]), it will caramelize very quickly, so keep watching it. At 338°F (170°C), it will turn amber; take it off the heat immediately, as it will keep cooking. Once it reaches over 350°F (180°C), it will turn a dark brown and taste bitter. If you are afraid that you can't cool the caramel in time, fill a sink with cool water before you start cooking and dip the bottom of the hot pan right away to cool the caramel. To clean caramel out of a pot, simply fill it with water to cover the caramel residue. Let it simmer for 10 minutes, and the caramel will dissolve.

Hot Water Bath—Bain Marie

The hot water bath method is commonly used to cook custards such as crème caramel and crème brûlée. It gently heats the custard so it doesn't overcook. Make sure your water is boiling hot, otherwise the custard will take a long time to cook. Tenting the pan with foil prevents a skin from forming on the top and preserves the velvety texture of your custard. Once the custard is ready, take it out of the hot water right away, otherwise it will continue to cook. If you leave it in the hot water, it may be overcooked and grainy.

FLAN PÂTISSIER

Flan pâtissier or Parisian flan is a custard baked in a flaky pastry shell. I have seen them at almost every bakery I've walked into in Paris. They are usually served in a big thick slice, wrapped up in a piece of paper to go. The burnt top makes it look unassuming, but it's where much of the flavor is. This pastry is so delicious that I find it hard to stop eating them—perhaps because they remind me of the Asian egg tarts that I grew up on. This is an advanced recipe where you will be preparing a pastry and a custard. The perfect flan pâtissier will be a test of making a flaky pastry and cooking a creamy custard, while baking it just the right amount of time. The result is well worth the time.

One recipe Pâte Brisée (page 16)

3 cups (720 g) whole milk

1 cup (250 g) whipping cream

1 vanilla bean, split and seeds scraped

4 large eggs, plus 1 yolk

¾ cup (150 g) granulated sugar

8 tbsp (70 g) cornstarch

½ tsp salt

3 tbsp (45 g) apricot jelly or strained apricot jam (optional)

Prepare the Pâte Brisée.

To make the custard, place the milk, whipping cream and vanilla pod and seeds into a medium pot over medium heat for about 2 to 3 minutes, until it starts to simmer. Turn off the heat, cover the pot and let it steep for 10 to 15 minutes. Do not boil the milk. Boiling the milk and cream may cause it to curdle; therefore, heat it just until it simmers.

Meanwhile, place the eggs and yolk into a medium bowl, and whisk in the sugar, cornstarch and salt until it is pale. Ladle about half of the hot milk into the eggs while whisking. Return the egg and milk mixture back to the pot with the rest of the milk. Take out the vanilla bean and cook the custard on medium heat, whisking continually for about 6 minutes, until bubbles break the surface.

Strain the custard into a clean container to remove any impurities from the eggs. It will be thick, so use a rubber spatula to press it through the strainer. Place a piece of plastic wrap directly on the custard's surface and let it cool completely. The custard needs to be completely cooled before using it. You can also make it up to 3 days in advance and store it in the refrigerator prior to assembling the tart.

To make the crust, line the bottom of an 8-inch (20-cm) round springform pan or a cake pan with a removable bottom with a piece of parchment paper. Roll out the Pâte Brisée dough to a 14-inch (36-cm) circle, then roll the dough around your rolling pin and gently unroll it into your cake pan. Carefully line the bottom and sides with the dough. Let it chill in the fridge for about 20 minutes. You can store this overnight and finish the rest the next day. It is best to rest the pastry dough after rolling and shaping it to minimize shrinkage.

(continued)

FLAN PÂTISSIER (CONTINUED)

Preheat the oven to 400°F (200°C). Take out the lined cake pan, and pour all the custard into the pastry. Smooth out the top with an offset spatula. With a pastry wheel or a paring knife, trim the crust ½ inch (13 mm) above the custard.

Place the flan on a baking sheet, and bake for 40 to 45 minutes—the center should be puffed up slightly and wobbly. Turn on the broiler and broil for 5 to 8 minutes to caramelize the top. Keep an eye on it, as it can burn very easily.

Take the flan out, and cool it completely for about 2 hours. Unmold it, and place it on a plate, wrap it tightly and let it set in the fridge overnight before serving. It is best served chilled or at room temperature. The custard in the flan is soft and creamy, so be sure to thoroughly chill it before cutting into it.

To glaze the flan, heat the apricot jelly or strained jam and gently brush it on the surface of the flan before serving. This will add a nice shine.

Unroll the pastry off the rolling pin onto the cake pan.

Line the bottom and sides of the pan.

Smooth the top with an offset spatula.

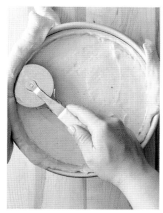
Trim the crust above the custard.

PLUM RASPBERRY CLAFOUTIS

Clafoutis is one of the easiest French desserts to make. Its texture is between custard and flan. It can be quite rustic, yet delicious. It is traditionally made with fresh cherries with their pits still inside so they can impart their unique almond flavor to the custard. If cherries are not in season, stone fruits such as plums and peaches would work just as well. I personally love the combination of plums and raspberries; their tartness is a beautiful contrast to the sweetness of the custard.

¼ cup (56 g) unsalted butter

2 cups (480 g) whole milk

¾ cup (150 g) granulated sugar, divided

1 vanilla bean, split and seeds scraped

4 large eggs

¼ tsp salt

½ cup (60 g) all-purpose flour

2 cups (300 g) plums, cut into small wedges (about 12 wedges per fruit)

1 cup (100 g) fresh raspberries

Powdered sugar, for dusting

In a small saucepan, melt the butter over medium heat. Continue cooking and swirling the pan for 3 to 4 minutes, until the butter turns light brown and aromatic. Set it aside to cool. The brown butter should be used in its liquid state, cooled or still lukewarm.

Preheat the oven to 350°F (180°C).

Place the milk, half the granulated sugar and the vanilla bean and seeds in a medium pot over medium heat until it simmers, about 3 minutes. Turn off the heat and cover the pot to let the milk steep while you prepare the rest of the recipe.

In a medium bowl, whisk together the eggs, salt and remaining sugar until it turns pale. Add the flour and whisk the mixture until it is no longer lumpy. Pour in the liquid brown butter and slowly incorporate it. Pour the mixture through a strainer into a clean container or bowl to remove any impurities.

Arrange the fruit on the bottom of a 9½-inch (24-cm) round, shallow dish such as a glass or ceramic pie dish. It doesn't have to be perfect. This dessert is meant to be a little rustic. Carefully pour the egg mixture over the fruit (the fruit will float to the top).

Place the dish on a baking sheet, and bake it for 50 to 60 minutes, until the custard sets. The edges should puff up a little and the center should no longer be liquid-like. Let the clafoutis cool. Dust the top with powdered sugar before serving. It is best served warm or at room temperature on the day it's baked.

> *Tip:* The brown butter is atypical in a clafoutis recipe, but it adds a nice depth of flavor. If you prefer, use melted butter instead.

EARL GREY CRÈME CARAMEL

My love for crème caramel started when I was an exchange student in Japan. Upon returning home, I was craving this delicious dessert, so I decided to make it at home, where I discovered that it is actually very easy to put together. The secret is to cook the caramel a little darker than you might think to get that unique flavor. The caramel then becomes a flavorful sauce for the smooth and rich custard. This is my twist on the classic crème caramel, but if you prefer just good old vanilla, leave out the tea.

Caramel

⅓ cup + 1 tbsp (80 g) granulated sugar

2 tbsp (30 g) water

Custard

1½ cups (360 g) whole milk

½ cup (120 g) whipping cream

1 vanilla pod, split and seeds scraped or 2 tsp (10 g) vanilla extract

2 tsp (3 g) whole Earl Grey tea leaves

½ cup (100 g) granulated sugar, divided

2 large eggs + 4 yolks

Tips: Cooking caramel is basically burning the sugar to a point where it doesn't taste bitter and unpalatable, which is why you shouldn't leave it unattended. Once your caramel reaches the right color and aroma, take it off the heat immediately as it will continue to cook and darken. I prefer my caramel a bit on the darker side, but it is up to you how dark to make it before it burns. For tips on making the perfect caramel, refer to page 48.

Preheat the oven to 300°F (150°C). Have a deep pan (such as a deep sheet cake pan) ready. Heat a kettle of water for a bain marie, or hot water bath.

While you make the caramel, line up your ramekins. In a small saucepan, add the sugar and water, and make sure the sugar is saturated with the water. Cook on medium-high heat, without stirring, swirling the pan every minute or so. The sugar will start to caramelize, but don't walk away, as it burns easily. Cook the caramel to a deep amber color, about 5 to 6 minutes. Quickly pour the caramel into the ramekins; be careful not to burn yourself, as the caramel is very hot. Swirl the cups to get the caramel even on the bottom and a bit on the edges. If the caramel becomes too firm to pour, gently heat it up on low.

To make the custard, place the milk, whipping cream, vanilla pod and seeds or extract, tea leaves and 2 tablespoons (30 g) of the sugar in a medium saucepan. Heat the milk mixture on medium heat until it simmers, about 4 minutes. Do not boil the milk. Turn off the heat, cover the pot and let the milk steep for 10 minutes.

Meanwhile, place the eggs, yolks and remaining sugar in a medium bowl, and whisk the mixture until it is pale, about a minute. Once the mixture is pale, as you whisk, slowly pour the hot milk into the eggs. Keep whisking until the mixture is incorporated.

Strain the custard into a clean container, preferably with a spout. Remove any air bubbles on the surface if necessary. Place the ramekins with the caramel in a deep baking dish or pan. Pour the custard into the ramekins and cover the pan with foil, leaving a corner for pouring the hot water. Place the baking dish on the oven rack and carefully pour the boiling water in the pan until it is half the height of the ramekins.

Bake for 25 minutes until the custards' centers are set. Carefully remove the foil to allow the steam to escape—the custard should jiggle in the middle if lightly agitated. With a dry dishtowel to protect your hands, slowly take out the ramekins and place them on a cooling rack. Cool them to room temperature, cover with plastic and place them in the fridge to chill overnight before serving. They can be refrigerated up to 3 days.

To serve, run a paring knife around the edge of the ramekin, and invert a plate on top. Carefully flip the ramekin and plate over. If the crème caramel doesn't come out, gently shake the ramekin to loosen it. Pour any remaining sauce over the custard.

CRÈME BRÛLÉE

Crème brûlée is the quintessential French dessert. Nothing is more satisfying when you break into the crunchy caramel to spoon out the creamy vanilla custard. It is easy to make, yet so delicious.

1¾ cups (420 g) whipping cream

¼ cup + 3 tbsp (100 g) whole milk

1 vanilla bean, split and seeds scraped

5 large egg yolks

2 tbsp + 2 tsp (40 g) granulated sugar, plus more for the tops

Preheat the oven to 300°F (150°C). Heat a kettle of water and prepare a pan, such as a deep cake pan, for a bain marie.

In a small saucepan, heat the cream, milk and vanilla pod and seeds on medium heat for 2 to 3 minutes until it simmers. Cover the pot and let the mixture steep for 10 to 15 minutes.

In a medium bowl, whisk together the egg yolks and sugar until pale and creamy. Slowly pour in the hot milk while whisking. Strain the liquid into a container such as a measuring cup with a spout.

Place four ¾-cup (180-ml) ramekins in a deep baking dish or pan and pour the custard into each ramekin. Skim off any surface bubbles if necessary. Place the baking dish onto the oven rack, and pour in hot water until it comes up about an inch (2.5 cm) below the ramekins. Loosely cover the top with foil.

Bake for 30 to 35 minutes. The center should jiggle slightly. Using a clean kitchen towel, transfer the ramekins to a cooling rack. Immediately remove the ramekins from the water, as they will continue to cook if left in the hot water. Wrap them in plastic and let them set in the fridge for at least 3 hours or overnight.

To serve, sprinkle a tablespoon (15 g) of sugar on each custard, and use a blowtorch to caramelize the tops. Let them cool so the caramel hardens before serving.

Tips: Most kitchen stores sell blowtorches for the home kitchen. You can also find them in hardware stores at a reasonable price.

I use dishes made for crème brûlée—shallow and wide. That way you can get a large surface area for the crunchy caramel. You can also use regular ramekins, and the custard is just as good.

CHOUX

Choux is a unique pastry where the liquid, butter and flour are cooked prior to the emulsification of eggs. As choux bakes, the eggs expand and release steam, creating a pocket that can be filled. Other pastries made from choux include the French cruller and churros. As long as you have a good sense of its consistency, you will have no problem making choux.

Making the Perfect Choux Paste

After you have added the flour to the liquid and butter, cook off some of the dough's moisture by cooking it in the pot and stirring it simultaneously to prevent burning. The drier dough can absorb the eggs more easily. The paste should look like dry mashed potatoes before adding the eggs and should be cooled to lukewarm. If the dough is too hot, the eggs may cook when you add them to the dough.

As you add the eggs, try to get a feel of the choux paste; when you lift the wooden spoon off the choux paste, the dough should form a soft peak. Add more eggs if the paste is too stiff. The finished choux paste should look shiny, and can hold its shape after being piped.

A common mistake in making choux paste is adding too much egg, making the finished product turn out flat and too soft to fill. Another one is under-baking; you have to let it bake long enough to develop a strong structure, and become dry enough to hold its shape.

Measure and lay out all the ingredients before starting.

The dough should look like dry mashed potatoes before adding the eggs.

Incorporate the eggs well after each addition.

The finished paste should be smooth and shiny.

PÂTE À CHOUX

Choux paste is a basic component to many classic pastries—éclairs, Paris-Brest, chouquettes, etc. The key to success is to dry out the dough before adding the eggs, and to adjust the amount of eggs in the paste to get the perfect consistency. If it's too wet, the choux will turn out flat. If it's too dry, the texture will be hard and dry.

¼ cup (60 g) water

¼ cup (60 g) whole milk

1 tbsp (15 g) granulated sugar

½ tsp salt

4 tbsp (60 g) unsalted butter, room temperature

½ cup (70 g) all-purpose flour

2½ large (125 g) eggs, well whisked

In a medium pot, bring the water, milk, sugar, salt and butter to a simmer over medium heat, about 3 minutes. Pour in the flour all at once, and vigorously stir with a wooden spoon to form a dough.

Keep it on medium heat and mix it to dry out the dough, about 4 minutes. The texture should look like dry mashed potatoes.

Take the pot off the heat and cool it for 5 minutes. This step is important because you are adding eggs next, and you don't want them to scramble. Add the eggs in three additions, stirring thoroughly after each addition. The choux paste should be shiny after incorporating the eggs.

Fill a piping bag fitted with a 1-centimeter round piping tip with the paste and pipe the dough per the pastry recipe you wish to make. Choux paste can be stored directly in the piping bag for up to 2 days in the fridge.

Tip: This recipe uses a combination of milk and water. The milk makes a tender pastry. You can swap out the milk for water to make a crispier pastry.

CHOUQUETTES AND CHOUX AU CRAQUELIN

⇒ Prep Time: 45 minutes - Makes 30 puffs ⇐

Chouquettes are nothing more than a choux pastry topped with pearl sugar, but they are something I find hard to stop eating. Perhaps because they are not filled, I snack on them like little cookies. In Paris, they are sold in bread bakeries; there's usually a basket full at the counter. The sweet and crunchy sugar is a wonderful contrast to the soft and custardy choux. Choux au craquelin are simply choux pastry topped with cookie-like disks baked on top. With this recipe, you can make either the chouquettes or crunchy puffs, or both!

1 batch Pâte à Choux (page 61)

Egg wash (1 egg yolk whisked with 1 tbsp [15 g] of water and a pinch of salt)

2 tbsp (30 g) pearl sugar

2½ tbsp (35 g) unsalted butter, room temperature

¼ cup (35 g) golden sugar

¼ cup (35 g) all-purpose flour

⅛ tsp salt

Preheat the oven to 400°F (200°C). Line two baking sheets with parchment paper.

To shape the choux paste, fill a piping bag fitted with a 1-centimeter round piping tip with the paste. Pipe 1-inch (2.5-cm) rounds. Hold your piping bag at a 90-degree angle to the baking tray, and keep a steady hand as you pipe. When the choux reaches the desired size, release the pressure on the piping bag and lift off the tip swiftly.

To make chouquettes, brush the choux lightly with the egg wash, and top them with the pearl sugar. Bake them for 5 minutes at 400°F (200°C). Lower the heat to 350°F (180°C) and bake for 20 to 22 minutes, until they are golden brown, rotating the baking sheets halfway through.

To make choux au craquelin, combine the butter, golden sugar, flour and salt in a small bowl and mix with a spatula. Roll the dough in between two pieces of parchment paper to about a ⅛-inch (3-mm) thickness. Place it on a baking tray and freeze it for about 15 minutes.

Take out the frozen cookie sheet, and cut out 1-inch (2.5-cm) rounds. Use an offset spatula to carefully lift off the rounds and set them on top of the piped choux paste. If they are too soft, return the cookie sheet to the freezer and try again.

Bake the puffs in the preheated oven at 400°F (200°C) for 5 minutes. Lower the heat to 350°F (180°C) and continue baking for 20 to 22 minutes, rotating the trays halfway through, until they are golden brown.

These choux puffs are best enjoyed warm and on the day they are baked.

GOUGÈRES

⇝ *Prep Time: 30 minutes - Makes 36 bite-size puffs* ⇜

Gougères are little cheese puffs made from choux paste. They are usually served as pre-dinner snacks with wine or drinks. But their crispy exteriors and tender, cheesy centers are so delicious, I would eat them any time of the day.

¼ cup (60 g) water

¼ cup (60 g) whole milk

1 tsp granulated sugar

1 tsp salt

4 tbsp (60 g) unsalted butter, room temperature

½ cup (70 g) all-purpose flour

2½ large (125 g) eggs, well whisked

1 cup (100 g) grated Gruyère cheese, plus more for garnish

¼ tsp freshly ground black pepper

Egg wash (1 egg yolk whisked with 1 tbsp [15 g] of water and a pinch of salt)

Smoked paprika (optional)

Preheat the oven to 400°F (200°C). Line two baking sheets with parchment paper.

In a medium pot, bring the water, milk, sugar, salt and butter to a simmer over medium heat, about 3 minutes. Pour in the flour all at once, and vigorously stir with a wooden spoon to form a dough.

Keep it on medium heat and mix it to dry out the dough, about 4 minutes. The texture should look like dry mashed potatoes.

Take the pot off the heat and cool it for 5 minutes. This step is important because you are adding eggs next, and you don't want them to scramble. Add the eggs in three additions, stirring thoroughly after each addition. The choux paste should be shiny after incorporating the eggs. Stir in the cheese and black pepper.

Fill a piping bag fitted with a 1-centimeter round piping tip with the paste. Pipe 1-inch (2.5-cm) rounds. Gently brush the tops with the egg wash and sprinkle with more cheese and the smoked paprika, if using.

Bake at 400°F (200°C) for 5 minutes, then lower the heat to 350°F (180°C). Continue baking for 20 to 22 more minutes, rotating the baking sheets halfway through, until they are golden brown.

Gougères are best served warm and on the day they are baked.

Tips: This recipe is based on the basic choux recipe (page 61) with minor adjustments in the seasoning.

Aged cheeses such as comté also work well in this recipe.

Baked gougères can be frozen in an airtight container for up to a week and reheated in a 300°F (150°C) oven for 5 to 10 minutes prior to serving.

COFFEE ÉCLAIRS

➔ *Prep Time: 1½ hours - Makes 20 éclairs* ❦

Éclairs are a pâtisserie staple; they come in all sorts of flavors, with chocolate and coffee being among the most popular. Their elongated shape makes them easy to eat and makes for a great shell-to-filling ratio. I prefer making small and narrow éclairs; they are so delicate. This advanced recipe has three components; it is very manageable if you make the filling a day ahead.

Base

1 batch Crème Pâtissière (page 11)

1 tbsp (3 g) freshly ground coffee beans

1 batch Pâte à Choux (page 61)

Egg wash (1 egg yolk whisked with 1 tbsp [15 g] of water and a pinch of salt)

Glaze

½ cup (80 g) white couverture chocolate, chopped

¼ cup (60 g) whipping cream

¼ cup + 2 tbsp (45 g) powdered sugar

½ tbsp (2 g) freshly ground coffee beans

Gold flakes, for garnish (optional)

Make the pastry cream following the recipe on page 11, but when infusing the milk, replace the vanilla bean and seeds with 1 tablespoon (3 g) of freshly ground coffee beans. Strain the custard and store in the fridge until necessary.

Preheat the oven to 400°F (200°C). Line two baking sheets with parchment paper.

Fill a piping bag with a 1-centimeter round tip with the pâte à choux. Pipe 4- to 5-inch (10- to 13-cm)-long lines, spaced 2 inches (3 cm) apart. Brush the tops lightly with egg wash. Éclairs can be tricky to pipe into straight lines. When you pipe them, don't apply too much pressure from the tip onto the paste. Instead, move slowly and let the paste land on the baking sheet. You can practice, then after piping scrape the paste back into your piping bag and start over.

Bake for 5 minutes, lower the heat to 350°F (180°C) and continue baking for 20 to 25 minutes more, rotating the baking sheets halfway through, until they are golden brown. They are done when they are hollow inside, and the walls shouldn't be too wet. Cool them completely before filling.

For the coffee glaze, melt the chocolate and whipping cream over a double boiler, being careful not to over-heat it. When it's melted, whisk in the powdered sugar and coffee. The glaze is best used at room temperature; if it is too warm it will melt off the éclairs.

Puncture three holes on the bottoms of the éclairs with a piping tip or a chopstick. Fill a piping bag with the coffee pastry cream and, with a small piping tip (about ¼ inch [6 mm] wide), fill the éclairs with the pastry cream through the three openings. Clean the bottoms with your finger. Repeat with the rest of the éclairs.

(continued)

To glaze the éclairs, make sure the glaze is at the right consistency; it shouldn't be too runny or too stiff. Try a test éclair and decide if you need to heat up the glaze or cool it down. Once you get the right temperature, carefully dip the top of an éclair, letting the excess slowly drip off. Clean off the sides of the glaze with your fingers if necessary. Repeat with the rest. Last, decorate with gold flakes if desired.

Tips: Traditionally the glaze is made with cooked fondant, which requires another step of sugar cooking. I have simplified the glaze recipe with more home-friendly ingredients and technique.

For white couverture chocolate, I use Valrhona Ivoire. Couverture chocolate is a high-quality chocolate containing a minimum of 30 percent cocoa butter. Since cocoa butter melts close to body temperature, couverture chocolate will have a melt-in-your-mouth texture. If you can't find couverture chocolate, substitute with the best-quality eating chocolate you can find, such as Lindt chocolate bars.

I have used ground espresso in the pastry cream for a bolder flavor. Some of the grinds may still be left in the pastry cream even after straining, but I like the texture they impart. If you prefer a smooth pastry cream, use a good-quality coffee extract instead. The same applies to the glaze; you can adjust the extract to taste.

GÂTEAU ST. HONORÉ

Prep Time: 2½ hours - Makes one 9-inch (23-cm) round cake

Gâteau St. Honoré is a unique cake made of puff pastry and a ring of choux, decorated with caramel choux puffs and crème Chantilly. It is named after Saint Honoré, the patron saint of pastry cooks, for whom a street in Paris is also named. This impressive dessert combines many textures of basic French pastry elements: choux, cream, puff pastry and crunchy caramel. Just like other puff pastry recipes, make sure you let the pastry rest after rolling to prevent shrinkage and deformation. Because this is an advanced pastry, I recommend making the puff, choux paste and pastry cream a day ahead. On the second day, you can focus on the assembly, a much easier approach.

¼ batch Traditional Pâte Feuilletée (page 95), or 1 sheet (300 g) frozen puff pastry

1 batch Pâte à Choux (page 61)

1 batch Crème Pâtissière (page 11)

1 cup (200 g) granulated sugar

¼ cup (60 g) water

2 tsp (10 g) lemon juice

1 batch Crème Chantilly (page 12), made right before using

To make the base, roll out the puff pastry to a 10-inch (25-cm) square, then let it rest for at least 2 hours, or overnight in the fridge. Preheat the oven to 400°F (200°C). Cut out a 9-inch (23-cm) circle, and dock the pastry with a fork evenly (see page 94).

Pipe a ring of choux paste along the edge, about 1 centimeter in. Pipe a second ring in the center, about 4 inches (10 cm). Bake for 10 minutes, then lower the heat to 350°F (180°C). Continue baking for 40 to 45 more minutes, until the pastry is golden brown. The choux should have good structure and not be too soft.

Pipe the remaining choux pastry into 1-inch (2.5-cm) rounds, about 12 to 16 balls. Bake them at 400°F (200°C) for 5 minutes, then lower the heat to 350°F (180°C). Continue baking for 15 to 20 more minutes, until they are golden brown. Cool the base and puffs before you fill them.

Whisk the pastry cream in a medium bowl to loosen it up. Fill a pastry bag with a narrow tip with about half of the pastry cream. Make a small hole in each choux puff and fill them with pastry cream. Reserve the rest of the pastry cream.

To make the caramel, combine the sugar, water and lemon juice in a clean medium saucepan, and cook over medium-high heat. Make sure the sugar is saturated with the water. Try not to stir the syrup; swirl the pan as you cook it. It should turn into a syrup and slowly caramelize. Once it turns amber, quickly dip the bottom of the pot in cold water to stop the caramel from burning. For a detailed explanation of cooking caramel, see page 48.

Carefully dip the tops of each filled puff in the caramel, and let them set on a clean tray.

(continued)

After all the tops are glazed, dip the bottom of each puff to glue them around the edge of the base. If the caramel has turned too hard, heat it on low for a minute or so to liquefy it again. You should fit about 12 puffs on the base.

Make the crème Chantilly, whipping the cream into firm peaks, and fill a pastry bag fitted with a St. Honoré tip. If you don't have one, use a plain or a star tip.

Transfer the pastry base onto a serving platter. Spread or pipe the reserved pastry cream over the inner ring. Pipe the crème Chantilly on top of the pastry cream, and place a filled puff in the center.

Gâteau St. Honoré is best served right after it is assembled. It will keep in the fridge for 2 to 3 hours, then the caramel will become soft.

Tips: This dessert is traditionally filled with chiboust cream—pastry cream lightened with meringue, which can be tricky to make. This more approachable recipe uses pastry cream and crème Chantilly.

To serve, slice the cake in between the puffs on the outer ring.

PARIS-BREST

⇒ *Prep Time: 1½ hours - Makes 10 (3-inch [8-cm]) cakes* ⇐

Paris-Brest was originally created to commemorate the Paris–Brest–Paris bicycle race, hence the pastry's wheel shape. It is a large choux pastry traditionally filled with a praliné mousseline, made with pastry cream, butter and praline paste. This smaller version is much easier to make and assemble. If you can't buy praline paste, use the recipe in the Basics section (page 20); it's so delicious that it is worth the trouble. Like the éclair recipe, this advanced recipe is more manageable if you make the pastry cream a day ahead.

1 batch Pâte à Choux (page 61)

Egg wash (1 egg yolk whisked with 1 tbsp [15 g] of water and a pinch of salt)

4 tbsp + 2 tbsp (30 g) crushed hazelnuts, divided

1 batch Crème Pâtissière (page 11)

½ cup (125 g) Hazelnut Praliné (page 20)

7 tbsp (100 g) unsalted butter, softened

Powdered sugar, to dust

Preheat the oven to 400°F (200°C). On a piece of parchment, mark ten 2½-inch (6-cm) round circles with a marker; this will be your template for piping the choux paste. Flip the paper onto a baking tray; the circles should be clearly visible.

Fill a piping bag with a 1-centimeter round or French star tip with choux paste. Pipe the paste following the marked circles. Lightly brush the egg wash onto their surfaces and top with 2 tablespoons (10 g) crushed hazelnuts.

Bake the choux for 5 minutes, then lower the temperature to 350°F (180°C) and bake for 35 to 40 more minutes. They are ready when golden brown, and their insides are no longer wet. Let the pastries cool completely before filling them.

To make the mousseline, beat the pastry cream in a medium bowl with a whisk until it's soft and creamy. Whisk in the praline paste until well combined. You don't want the cream to be too cold before you add the butter, otherwise the butter will seize into small chunks in the mousseline. The butter should be soft when you add it to the cream. Whisk until the mixture is creamy and blended. Fill a piping bag with a star or plain tip with the mousseline, and set it aside until you are ready to fill the pastries.

To assemble the pastries, slice them in half as you would for a sandwich. Pipe the mousseline on the bottom half, and place the top half back on. Decorate the sides with the remaining crushed hazelnuts. Repeat with the rest of the pastries. Dust the tops lightly with powdered sugar before serving.

These are best served they day they are made. They will keep in the fridge for up to 2 days in an airtight container.

Tip: Praline paste is a caramelized nut paste and is available in some specialty food stores, but you can also make it at home.

⇶ TARTS ⇷

Tarts are easily one of my favorite French desserts. They are a wonderful marriage of different textures and flavors—buttery tart shells, seasonal fruits, nuts, cream, the list goes on. The simple Tarte au Citron, lemon tart (page 83), is a classic that can be found in almost every bakery in Paris, but tarts can also be incredibly intricate and complex.

Every tart starts with a pastry base, a foundation for the delicious fillings. Don't be intimidated if you haven't made one from scratch. Think of these bases as cookie or pie dough. The process is not difficult and with a little precision and practice, you can achieve bakery-quality tarts at home.

The two basics you'll need are Pâte Brisée (page 16) and Pâte Sucrée (page 15). Pâte brisée is a flaky dough suitable for pastries such as Quiche Lorraine (page 91) and Tarte aux Pommes (page 84). It is good for tarts with a sweet filling or when your tart needs a sturdy crust. It can be blind-baked or baked from raw dough with the filling. Pâte sucrée translates to "sweet paste." It is a sweet-tart dough that is usually rolled thin, shaped into the tart crust and blind-baked.

Once you've mastered the methods to make different pastry bases and fillings, you can put your creative twist on them and make your own versions.

What Size Should the Dough Be Rolled Out To?

The size and depth of your tart pans or rings will help you determine this. For example, if your tart ring is 9 inches (23 cm) in diameter, and 1 inch (2.5 cm) deep, you will need to roll out the dough to the pan's diameter plus 2 inches (5 cm) for the sides, plus a overhang of at least 1 inch (2.5 cm) to trim. That means your dough needs to be about 12 inches (30 cm) in diameter to fit in the tart pan with a little overhang. See page 74, images 1 and 2.

On Blind-Baking

Several of this book's recipes require blind-baking tart shells made from pâte sucrée, especially if you are filling them with a fresh filling. Here are some guidelines on blind-baking.

Roll out the dough to the desired thickness. Keep in mind the texture: generally, smaller tart shells should be thinner (2 to 3 mm) while large tart shells are thicker (3 to 4 mm) as they require more structure.

To blind-bake, preheat the oven to 350°F (180°C). Line the chilled tart dough in its pan with paper baking cups or parchment paper. Then weigh down the dough with beans or rice (page 74, images 3 through 6). I like using mung beans as they are cheap, and are small enough to get into the edge of the tarts.

It is important to chill the tart dough for about 20 minutes before you line them with the paper and beans, and then again before you bake them.

Bake the tarts for about 30 minutes, until the edges turn slightly golden. If you under-bake them at this stage, they might be misshapen because they haven't had a chance to set properly. When the tarts are cool to the touch, carefully remove the paper and beans (page 74, image 7). Lower the oven temperature to 325°F (160°C), and bake them for 15 to 25 more minutes, depending on their size and thickness. They should be evenly golden brown throughout (page 74, images 8 and 9).

> *Tip:* Roll out the dough as evenly as you can, so the tart shell bakes evenly. If the tart dough becomes too soft, place it in the fridge to firm it up before working with it again.

MANGO RASPBERRY SABLÉ BRETON TART

⇛ *Prep Time: 1 hour* - *Makes one 8-inch (20-cm) round tart* ⇚

A delicious twist on the Sablé Breton (page 25), a traditional cookie becomes the base for this tart. It is filled with vanilla pastry cream and topped with fresh mangoes and raspberries. The tart is similar to one made with pâte sucrée, but thicker and more tender and crumbly.

1 recipe Sablé Breton dough (page 25) + egg wash

1 recipe Crème Pâtissière (page 11)

½ lb (225 g) fresh mangoes, cut into ½-inch (13-mm) cubes

Lime juice and zest (optional)

½ cup (50 g) fresh raspberries

Preheat the oven to 350°F (180°C). Line the bottom of an 8-inch (20-cm) cake ring, springform pan or cake pan with a removable bottom with parchment and set it aside until you are ready to use.

If the sablé dough is cold, take it out of the fridge and bring it to room temperature for 15 to 20 minutes, until it is soft enough to roll. On a lightly dusted work surface, roll out the dough to 10 inches (25 cm); it should be about ½ inch (13 mm) thick. Trace and cut out an 8-inch (20-cm) circle for the base. Place the dough onto the bottom of the prepared cake pan.

Brush the top of the sablé with the egg wash and bake it for 30 to 35 minutes until the edge and top are golden brown. Let it cool, take it out of the pan and gently peel off the parchment paper. If you are not assembling the tart that day, tightly wrap it in plastic wrap for up to 3 days at room temperature.

To assemble the tart, fit a piping bag with a 1-centimeter round piping tip and fill it with vanilla pastry cream. If desired, toss the mango chunks with a tablespoon (15 g) of lime juice and a teaspoon of lime zest. This will keep them tasting fresh for longer. Place the sablé base on a serving platter. Pipe the pastry cream onto the base, and garnish with mango chunks and raspberries. Serve immediately. It is best served the day it is made.

> *Tip:* You can make the base and pastry cream up to 2 days ahead. Prepare the mangoes and assemble the tart right before you serve it.

CHOCOLATE GANACHE TART

≫ Prep Time: 1 hour - Makes one 8-inch (20-cm) round tart ≪

This is another easy-to-assemble dessert that is quite decadent. The filling barely requires cooking.
To make a delicious and smooth chocolate ganache, start with high-quality couverture chocolate.
Couverture chocolate contains at least 30 percent cocoa butter, which is why it is more expensive and
melts so nicely on the tongue. Each brand makes them in different shapes, so measuring in grams will
be the most accurate. I have not tried this recipe using baking chocolate or eating chocolate,
which will likely have very different results.

1 recipe Pâte Sucrée (page 15), blind-baked into an 8-inch (20-cm) tart shell

½ cup + 1 tbsp (80 g) dark chocolate, chopped (preferably Valrhona Alpaco 65 percent)

½ cup + 1 tbsp (80 g) milk chocolate, chopped (preferably Valrhona Jivara 40 percent)

1 tbsp (15 g) liquid honey

½ cup + 3 tbsp (160 g) whipping cream

½ tsp salt

1 tbsp (15 g) unsalted butter, room temperature

1 tbsp (8 g) cocoa nibs, for garnish

Gold flakes, for garnish

Bake a tart shell or use a pre-baked tart shell (see instructions for blind-baking on page 76). Place the chopped chocolates and honey in a medium bowl and set it aside.

In a small saucepan, warm the cream over medium heat until it starts to simmer, about 2 minutes. Pour the hot cream into the chocolate-honey mixture, and cover the bowl with a piece of plastic. Let it sit for 3 to 4 minutes, allowing the cream's heat to melt the chocolate. With a rubber spatula, start mixing in small circles in the middle, and slowly work in larger circles until the chocolate and cream are emulsified. Add the salt and butter, and mix until incorporated.

Pour the liquid ganache into the tart shell. It can set at room temperature, depending on how warm it is. You can also let it set in the fridge for 20 to 30 minutes.

To garnish, sprinkle it with cocoa nibs and gold flakes or serve the tart with a light dusting of cocoa powder.

Tips: The tart will keep in the fridge for up to 2 days, but is best served when the ganache has just set. The ganache may shrink slightly and crack if chilled overnight, and the tart shell will start to soften from the moisture in the ganache.

A chocolate ganache is usually an emulsion of cream and chocolate. To emulsify the water and fat in the ganache, avoid boiling or over-heating the cream. It can cause the ganache to "split," the fat separating from the rest of the ganache. Sometimes cooling it and adding a touch of liqueur or water then mixing it vigorously or blending it with an immersion blender can fix this. In contrast, if your cream was not hot enough, some chocolate pieces may still be solid. This can be easily fixed by briefly heating the bowl in a double boiler, only until the rest of the chocolates are melted.

TARTE AU CITRON

Tarte au citron is another French bakery staple. Every bakery has its own version of this sweet tart shell filled with lemon curd. There are an endless number of recipes for lemon curd, but they all have similar ingredients—eggs, sugar, lemon juice and butter in different ratios. This recipe has lots of butter, which makes it silky and rich. The trick is incorporating the butter with a blender.

1 recipe Pâte Sucrée (page 15), blind-baked into six 3-inch (8-cm) round tarts

2 large eggs + 1 yolk

½ cup + 2 tsp (110 g) granulated sugar

¼ cup + 3 tbsp (100 g) lemon juice (about 3 large lemons)

2 tsp (4 g) finely grated lemon zest (about 1 large lemon)

10 tbsp (140 g) unsalted butter, room temperature, cut into small chunks

Finely grated lime zest, for garnish

Edible flowers, for garnish (optional)

For the crust, pre-bake the pâte sucrée (see instructions for blind-baking on page 76). In a medium bowl, whisk together the eggs, yolk and sugar until it becomes pale. Gently whisk in the lemon juice and zest.

Transfer the mixture to a small saucepan and cook it over medium heat, slowly mixing with a silicone spatula. Make sure to stir the entire bottom of the pot so the curd doesn't burn. The mixture will start to curdle in about 4 to 5 minutes, at 195°F (90°C). When you are cooking the lemon curd, be sure to keep stirring with your spatula to prevent burning. Since this recipe makes a small batch, it will cook very quickly. If it burns, you will need to start over.

Take it off the heat, and strain the mixture into a clean, heatproof, medium bowl to remove the zest and any impurities. With an immersion blender, blend in the butter 1 tablespoon (15 g) at a time. Scrape down the sides of the bowl. Place a piece of plastic wrap directly on the curd's surface, and chill it for at least 2 hours, or overnight.

When you're ready to assemble it, whisk the chilled lemon curd to loosen it to a mayonnaise-like consistency. Spoon the curd into the baked tart shells and, using a small offset spatula, gently level off the excess curd by pushing the spatula away from you. Repeat the process with the rest of the tarts. If the curd is very soft, you can let the tarts set in the fridge for about 30 minutes before garnishing and serving.

To garnish, grate lime zest on top and decorate with the edible flowers. They are best served the day they are made, and can be kept in the fridge for up to 2 days.

> **Tip:** Since this lemon curd recipe has a generous amount of butter, it is best to emulsify the fat with a blender (very much like making a mayonnaise). This way the curd will be extra smooth, creamy and less likely to separate. Be sure to blend in the butter while the curd is still hot, otherwise the butter will not melt easily.

TARTE AUX POMMES

⇒ Prep Time: 1 hour - Makes one 9-inch (23-cm) round tart ⇐

Tarte aux pommes, also known as French apple tart, is made with a flaky pastry, fresh apple slices dotted with butter and sugar to finish. Without spices or brown sugar, this tart showcases the buttery pastry and delicious fruit. For a more rustic version, try making a free-form tart without the pan.

1 recipe Pâte Brisée (page 16)

4 medium Granny Smith apples, peeled, cored and cut into ⅛-inch (3-mm)-thick slices

2 tbsp (30 g) fresh lemon juice (about half of a large lemon)

3 tbsp (45 g) unsalted butter, room temperature

½ cup (100 g) granulated sugar

3 tbsp (45 g) apricot jelly or strained apricot jam

Roll out the pâte brisée to a 13-inch (33-cm) circle. Transfer the dough into a 9-inch (23-cm) fluted tart pan with a removable bottom. Gently push the dough into the bottom, edges and corners. Remove the excess dough by rolling the top of the pan with a rolling pin. Let the crust rest in the fridge while you make the filling.

Preheat the oven to 400°F (200°C).

Peel, core and slice the apples into ⅛-inch (3-mm)-thick slices. Place the slices in a large bowl and toss them with the lemon juice.

Arrange the apple slices in the chilled pastry shell, fitting in as many as you can; the apples will shrink as they bake. Dot the apples with butter, and sprinkle the sugar evenly all over them. Bake for 45 to 50 minutes, until the pastry turns golden brown and the apples are caramelized on the edges. Cool the tart slightly before taking it out of the pan.

Warm the apricot jelly, and gently brush it on the top of the apples. The tart is best served the day it is baked and will keep in the fridge for up to 2 days.

Tips: You can arrange the apple slices in any pattern you like—be creative!

To make a free-form tart, simply skip lining the pastry in the pan. Arrange the apples in the center of the rolled-out dough, and fold up the edges of the pastry. You may need to decrease the bake time for this method.

FRANGIPANE PEAR TART

⇒ *Prep Time: 1 to 1½ hours* - *Makes one 9-inch (23-cm) round tart* ⇐

The almond pear tart is a French classic, filled with almond frangipane, and topped with fresh or poached pears. For simplicity, this recipe uses freshly sliced pears. This is an excellent example of how versatile the basic recipes are; starting with the simple tart dough (page 15) and frangipane (page 19) recipes, you can create an array of desserts such as this delicate and delicious pear tart. Berries and stone fruits such as plums also work exceptionally well. You can blind-bake the tart a day ahead and assemble it the next day. You can also use a premade tart shell if you are pressed for time, but homemade is recommended.

1 recipe Pâte Sucrée (page 15), blind-baked into a 9-inch (23-cm) tart shell

1 recipe Almond Frangipane (page 19)

3 ripe but firm pears, thinly sliced (Anjou pears work well)

3 tbsp (45 g) apricot jelly or strained apricot jam

Crème Chantilly (page 12), for serving (optional)

For the crust, pre-bake the pâte sucrée (see instructions for blind-baking on page 76).

Preheat the oven to 375°F (190°C).

Leave your baked tart shell inside the ring or tart pan. When you bake the tart with the filling, it will expand, so the tart ring will keep your pastry in shape. Pipe or fill the shell with the frangipane using an offset spatula. Level off the frangipane and top with the sliced pears. I did the classic design of fanned slices, but you can arrange them to your liking.

Bake for about 40 minutes, rotating the pan halfway through. It is done when the top of the frangipane is a golden color. To glaze, heat the apricot jelly and gently brush it on the surface of the flan. Cool the tart before serving. It is also delicious served with a side of Crème Chantilly (page 12) or vanilla ice cream.

> *Tip:* When you are blind-baking your tart shell for this recipe, under-bake it a little. Since you will be baking it again with the filling, if you baked it to the perfect color, it might turn out too dark after the second baking.

FRESH FIG AND ORANGE TARTS

⇉ *Prep Time: 1 to 1½ hours - Makes four 4-inch (10-cm) round fluted tarts* ⇇

Fresh fruit tart is one of my favorite desserts. The fun thing about making them at home is that you can let yourself be creative. Here I have infused the pastry cream with cinnamon and orange, and used fresh figs and oranges. Using this recipe as inspiration, you can infuse different flavors and use seasonal fruits to make your own version. Bake the shell and make the pastry cream a day ahead, so all you need to do is to assemble it before you serve. You can also use a premade tart shell if you are in a pinch, but homemade is always recommended.

1 recipe Pâte Sucrée (page 15), blind-baked into four 4-inch (10-cm) fluted round tarts

1¼ cups (300 g) whole milk

4½ tbsp (68 g) granulated sugar, divided

¼ vanilla bean, split and seeds scraped

4-inch (10-cm) cinnamon stick

4 egg yolks

3 tbsp (25 g) cornstarch

A pinch of salt

2 tbsp (30 g) unsalted butter, softened

2 tsp orange zest

1 lb (454 g) fresh brown figs, halved or quartered, for garnish

2 medium oranges, sectioned and cut into bite-size pieces, for garnish

Prepare the pâte sucrée (see instructions for blind-baking on page 76). To make the pastry cream, heat the milk in a small saucepan over medium heat with 2 tablespoons (30 g) of sugar, the vanilla bean and seeds and the cinnamon stick until it starts to simmer. Turn off the heat, cover the pot and let it steep.

In a medium bowl, whisk together the egg yolks, remaining sugar, cornstarch and salt. Slowly pour in the hot milk while whisking the egg mixture. Return the mixture to the pot, and, over medium heat, keep whisking the mixture to avoid burning it, for about 3 to 4 minutes. The custard will start to thicken, and when it starts to boil, it is ready.

Take the pot off the heat, whisk in the butter and strain the custard into a clean bowl. Stir in the orange zest. Last, place a piece of plastic wrap directly onto the surface of the custard, cool and store it in the fridge for at least 2 hours. This can be made up to 3 days in advance.

To assemble the tarts, spoon or pipe the pastry cream into the baked tart shells, filling them to the top. Arrange the figs and oranges on top. Serve right away or keep it in the refrigerator. They are best served the day they are assembled.

Tips: To keep your tart shells crunchy, you can bake the shells up to 2 days ahead, store them in an airtight container and assemble them right before serving.

Avoid using fruits that have high water contents; they usually release too much moisture when assembled.

QUICHE LORRAINE

I was surprised to see so many quiche options when I visited Paris for the first time. There were usually at least three large ones baked and sliced on the counter at the neighborhood bakery. Quiche Lorraine is named after the Lorraine region in France, and is traditionally made with lardons, cheese and cream. Because this is an advanced recipe, I recommend making the pastry a day or two ahead. That way you just need to prepare the filling on the day of serving.

1 recipe Pâte Brisée (page 16)

10 to 15 slices (200 g) smoked bacon, cut into ¼-inch (6-mm) chunks

5 large eggs

2 cups (500 g) whipping cream

1 tsp salt

¼ tsp freshly cracked black pepper

¼ tsp ground nutmeg

1 cup (100 g) grated Gruyère cheese

Roll out the pâte brisée to a 13-inch (33-cm) round. Line a 9-inch (23-cm) round quiche pan with the pastry. Trim the excess dough, and let the crust rest in the fridge for at least 30 minutes before filling it.

Preheat the oven to 400°F (200°C). In a frying pan, fry the bacon over medium heat until it turns golden, about 5 minutes. Drain off the excess fat and set it aside until necessary.

In a medium bowl, whisk the eggs, cream and seasonings until well combined. Place the bacon and grated cheese onto the lined pastry, and set the pan on a baking tray. Pour the egg mixture over the filling, making sure the bacon and cheese are submerged in the liquid. Bake the quiche for 40 to 45 minutes, until the filling is golden and the middle has puffed up slightly. It should be soft in the center. Take out the quiche and let it cool before serving.

Tips: Traditional quiche Lorraine is made without onions, but you can add onions or substitute other ingredients if you wish.

Be sure not to overfill the quiche with the eggs, as the crust will shrink and the filling may overflow as it bakes.

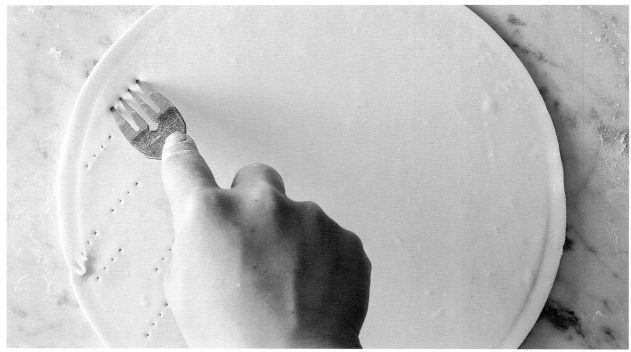

PÂTE FEUILLETÉE

There is nothing more gratifying for a baker than to master the art of pâte feuilletée, puff pastry. If you have the time, I strongly recommend making a big batch and storing it in the freezer for later use. Homemade is simply the best. If you choose to use frozen puff pastry, make sure you buy an all-butter pastry. If you know a good bakery that makes their puff pastry in-house, they might be willing to sell you a small portion.

A Note on Butter

If making your own puff pastry, use a butter containing at least 82 percent milk fat, such as European-style butter. Generally speaking, butter with a higher fat content is easier to laminate (see page 149) and will result in a flakier pastry. Puff pastry puffs because the butter gives off steam during the baking process, so the more even layers of butter, the better the pastry is. Since a large portion of the pastry is made with butter, make sure you use the best quality you can find.

On Using Puff Pastry

To use frozen puff pastry (homemade or store-bought), thaw the pastry several hours in the fridge. Never store it at room temperature because the butter might become too warm and the layers will not be defined as it melts out.

Depending on the size of your frozen pastry, you may need to combine sheets if they are too small for what you want to use it for. To combine them, brush the top of one sheet lightly with water, stack another sheet on top, then roll it to the desired thickness and size.

Always roll your puff pastry cold from the fridge; this way the butter and layers will stay intact. Resting is always necessary after you roll your pastry as the gluten bonds will shrink when they are tight. If you skip this step, the pastry may shrink and deform in unexpected ways. The pastry also may not be tender or puff up as much as it should.

Most of the recipes require docking the pastry after it is rolled out, that is, piercing the dough with small holes using a fork or docking wheel. The holes let the steam escape in the baking process so the pastry rises in an even layer. This is especially important when making Mille-Feuille (page 107) because you want the dough to be one level sheet before you assemble the pastries.

TRADITIONAL PÂTE FEUILLETÉE

⇒ *Prep Time: 2 to 3 hours - Makes 2¾ pounds (1.2 kg) of pastry* ⇐

Pâte feuilletée can be laborious, but the result is absolutely worthwhile. While you can find good-quality store-bought pastry, it simply can't beat a well-made homemade one. It is amazing how five ingredients can transform into a buttery and delicately layered pastry. Allowing enough time to let the pastry rest in between turns is the key to success. This recipe yields a big batch. The time it takes to make a small and a large batch of pastry is roughly the same, so I usually make more than I need, which I can freeze and save for later use.

1⅓ cups (500 g) all-purpose flour

1 tbsp + 1 tsp (20 g) fine salt

5 tbsp (75 g) unsalted butter, softened

1 cup (250 g) cold water

1 tbsp (15 g) white vinegar

1¾ cups + 2 tbsp (425 g) unsalted butter

In a mixing bowl, whisk together the flour and salt. Add the butter, water and vinegar. Mix on low speed for 5 minutes, until a cohesive dough forms. Wrap the dough in plastic wrap and let it rest in the fridge for at least 4 hours before proceeding with the turns.

To prepare the butter, make a pack using parchment paper. Fold the paper into a roughly 6-inch (15-cm) square and place the butter in the center. You will be rolling the butter into a 6-inch (15-cm) square pack. Fold in the edges around it and roll it into an even sheet. Chill the butter in the fridge until you are ready to use it.

In pastry lamination (layering pastry dough with butter, see page 149), a "turn" is whenever we fold a sheet of pastry. There are two types of folds—single or letter folds, and double or book folds. Traditional puff pastry takes at total of 6 single folds. In between every 2 folds, the pastry needs to rest so the gluten bonds can relax, which makes it easier to work with. After all these folds and turns, the finished pastry will have more than 700 layers!

When you are ready to laminate, make sure the butter consistency is as close to the dough as possible. You may need to bring it to room temperature for 15 minutes, and roll it with a rolling pin to soften it.

I do not recommend heating butter in the microwave oven for lamination; it overheats too easily. Lamination is all about temperature; the butter and dough should be cool, but not so firm that it is difficult to roll or that the butter cracks. If it is too warm, the butter may leak out of the dough, which will yield poor lamination.

(continued)

Roll the dough into a 10-inch (25-cm) square, and turn it 45 degrees so it faces you as a diamond shape. Unwrap the softened butter from the parchment pack, and place it in the center, leaving triangles of dough on four sides. Fold the triangles of dough around the butter and pinch the edges closed to make a sealed pack.

Dust the dough and work surface with flour if necessary. Roll the dough and butter out to roughly 9 x 18 inches (23 x 43 cm). Fold it into thirds like a business letter. Make the first turn: turn the dough 90 degrees, and repeat the rolling and folding process. You have now finished the second fold. Wrap the dough in plastic, and let it rest in the fridge for at least an hour.

Repeat the rolling and folding steps above two more times, which will be a total of 6 folds and turns. Mark the number of folds with a piece of tape so you know how many folds you have completed.

After the final turn, wrap the dough in plastic and chill it overnight. At this point the gluten bonds in the dough are very tight from the turning and rolling, so it needs to relax before you can use it for pastries. Without adequate resting time, the pastry may shrink or turn out flat.

The finished puff pastry dough is best kept in the freezer, well wrapped, for 1 to 2 months. Let it thaw in the fridge before using it. Never store puff pastry at room temperature.

Tips: Vinegar increases the dough's malleability as well as slows down its oxidization and discoloration.

The main reasons to rest the dough are the gluten and the butter. Rolling and folding the dough makes the gluten bonds stronger. The butter inside will also become softer. Without time to chill, the dough will be very tough to roll, and the soft butter will make the layers less defined.

Allow the dough to rest before proceeding with two turns.

Make a butter pack by wrapping it in parchment paper and rolling it.

Roll out the corners of the dough and place the butter in the center.

Make a single fold (letter fold).

Turn the dough 90 degrees before making the second roll and fold.

Make the second single fold (letter fold). Let the dough rest before making more turns.

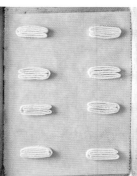

PALMIERS

⇾ *Prep Time: 30 minutes - Makes 12 to 18 palmiers* ⇽

Palmiers are one of my favorite puff pastry "cookies." They are simply puff pastry rolled in sugar and folded. As they bake they puff up and turn into palm leaf shapes. Another name for these is elephant ears. These crispy, caramelized, thin pastries are so irresistible. I like to bake them to an amber color for the caramel flavor, but keep an eye on them during the last few minutes of baking, as they burn quickly.

¼ batch Traditional Pâte Feuilletée (page 95), or 1 sheet (300 g) frozen puff pastry

½ cup (100 g) granulated sugar, divided

Tip: Palmiers are one of those simple pastries that can be hard to master. When you roll out the pastry, the size and thickness might make them turn out perfectly or unravel completely. I have experimented with store-bought and homemade puff pastry, and they yield completely different results. You may have to do a bit of experimentation to see what works. Regardless, they will all turn out to be delicious caramelized, buttery pastries!

Preheat the oven to 400°F (200°C). Line two baking sheets with parchment paper.

If your puff pastry is frozen, thaw it in the fridge for 2 hours or overnight before using it. Sprinkle sugar on your work surface and on the puff pastry, sprinkling more as needed.

The final size should be about 8 x 16 inches (20 x 40 cm). If you are using homemade pastry, roll it to roughly 9 x 18 inches (23 x 46 cm), and trim it to the desired size. If you are using frozen puff pastry, it is usually already trimmed, so you just need to roll it to the final size.

It is important that the thickness of the pastry is about 2½ to 3 millimeters, otherwise the palmiers tend to unravel as they bake. You may roll it to a wider width (not length, as this would change the shape), depending on how big your pastry is. Make sure the thickness is even. If your pastry sheet is larger, you will get more palmiers.

Once the dough is rolled to the desired size, spread the remaining sugar evenly on the pastry, as you want each palmier to have similar sweetness and caramelization.

Mark the halfway point in the dough, lengthwise, either by measuring (about 8 inches [20 cm]) or folding the sheet in half and then unfolding it. From the edges, fold each half of the pastry sheet in thirds, toward the center. Try to roll the pastry as evenly as you can for the most consistent shape and baking.

Finally, fold the pastry in half, with the folds inside. With a sharp knife, cut the pastry into about ¼-inch (6-mm)-thick pieces, trimming off the two ends if necessary.

Place the pastries cut-side up on the baking trays, about 2½ inches (6 cm) apart; the palmiers expand quite a bit as they bake.

Bake them one tray at a time for 15 minutes, take them out and carefully flip each one with an offset spatula. Return them to the oven and bake them for 5 to 8 more minutes, until they are evenly caramelized and golden. If they brown too quickly, lower the heat to 325°F (160°C) to finish baking. Cool them completely before storing them. They keep well in an airtight container for up to a week.

CHAUSSON AUX POMMES

Chausson aux pommes is a classic French breakfast pastry, much like an apple turnover. It is made with buttery puff pastry and filled with apple compote or chunks. Most versions I have tasted in Paris are not spiced, but I have used a little cinnamon because I love the flavor. The scoring part is the most fun; make sure you rest and chill the pastries thoroughly before you score them to get a clean pattern.

½ batch Traditional Pâte Feuilletée (page 95), or 1 sheet (300 g) frozen puff pastry

1 tbsp (15 g) unsalted butter

3 medium (300 g) Granny Smith apples, diced

¼ cup (35 g) brown sugar

¼ tsp ground cinnamon

1 tsp rum (optional)

Egg wash (1 egg yolk whisked with 1 tbsp [15 g] of water and a pinch of salt)

Simple syrup, for brushing (optional)

If you are using it frozen, thaw the puff pastry in the fridge for 2 hours or overnight before using it. In a small saucepan, brown the butter over medium heat, about a minute. Add the apples, and toss them in the brown butter. Then add the brown sugar, and cook it for 3 to 4 minutes, until the apples soften but still hold their shape. Finish them with the cinnamon and rum, if using. Cool the apples before filling the pastries.

Dust your work surface and pastry with flour. Roll out the puff pastry to roughly 14 x 11 inches (36 x 28 cm) and cut out six 4½-inch (11.5-cm) rounds. You can use the top of a fluted tart pan as a cutter or a bowl or a small plate to trace the rounds. Roll out each pastry to about 7-inch (18-cm) ovals. Roll the pastry thinner in the center, leaving the edges thicker. This will give you enough area to fold the pastry over when filled and ensure the pastries don't unfold as they bake. The thickness of the pastry should be about ¹⁄₁₆ of an inch or less (1 to 2 mm).

Place a heaping tablespoon (30 g) of filling onto the center of each pastry. Brush the bottom-half edge with egg wash and fold the pastry in half to form a half-moon shape. Press down the edges to seal in the filling. Place them on a parchment-lined baking tray. Loosely cover the pastries with plastic, and let them rest in the fridge for 1 to 2 hours or overnight. You can also freeze them to bake later.

Preheat the oven to 400°F (200°C).

While the pastries are cold, brush a thin layer of egg wash on the top. With a sharp paring knife, score a leaf pattern on each pastry and make a small incision into each for the steam to escape.

Bake them for 30 to 35 minutes, until the tops are golden brown. Brush them with simple syrup while they are hot, if desired.

GALETTE DES ROIS

Prep Time: 1 hour - Makes one 9-inch (23-cm) round galette

Galette des rois is also known as a pithivier. I have seen them in every single bakery I have walked into in Paris during early January. They are made of puff pastry filled with almond frangipane. The name means "king's cake" and it is served on Epiphany in France. The fun of it is in the fève, a charm that is hidden inside. When the slices are shared among your family and friends, the person who gets the fève is the king or queen for the day.

½ batch Traditional Pâte Feuilletée (page 95), or 1½ lbs (600 g) frozen puff pastry

1 batch Almond Frangipane (page 19), ready to use in a piping bag

A charm or bean, if desired

Egg wash (1 egg yolk whisked with 1 tbsp [15 g] of water and a pinch of salt)

¼ cup (60 ml) simple syrup, for brushing (optional)

If your puff pastry is frozen, thaw it in the fridge for 2 hours or overnight before using it. If the pastry is in one sheet, divide it into two equal sheets. Dust the work surface with flour, and roll one piece into a 12-inch (30-cm) square. Place a plate or cake pan on it and use it as a guide to cut out a 10-inch (25-cm) round. Repeat this process with the remaining pastry sheet.

Place one pastry sheet on a parchment-lined baking sheet. Pipe the frangipane onto the center of the pastry, leaving a 1-inch (2.5-cm) edge. Spread the frangipane evenly if necessary. If you wish, place a charm or a bean on the frangipane. Brush the edge with egg wash, and carefully place the remaining sheet of pastry over the filled sheet. Gently press the edges to seal in the filling. It is best to rest the pastry in the fridge for at least 2 hours or overnight before baking it to prevent shrinkage.

Preheat the oven to 400°F (200°F). Crimp the edge of the pastry with your fingers and the back of a paring knife, if desired. Brush the top evenly with egg wash, and score a pattern on it with the tip of a paring knife.

Bake for 35 to 40 minutes, rotating the baking sheet halfway through, until the top is a rich golden color. Brush it with simple syrup while it's hot, if desired.

It is best served the day it is baked. You can also reheat it in a 300°F (150°C) oven for 10 minutes to refresh it before serving.

Tips: There are many kinds of patterns you can score on the galette; it is up to you how intricate you want it to be.

The pastry is best baked when it is cold, taken right out of the fridge.

TARTE TATIN

Tarte tatin is a must-make when it comes to French pastry. The name comes from Hotel Tatin in Lamotte-Beuvron, France, where it was created. Think of it as an upside-down apple pie with a buttery caramel sauce on the bottom, fresh apples and puff pastry baked on top, which is then inverted onto a platter to serve. Be sure to cook the caramel to a deep amber color to get the most flavor.

¼ batch Traditional Pâte Feuilletée (page 95), or 1 sheet (300 g) frozen puff pastry

6 medium Granny Smith apples, peeled, cored and cut into quarters

2 tbsp (30 g) lemon juice, divided

½ cup (100 g) granulated sugar

6 tbsp (85 g) unsalted butter, room temperature

½ vanilla bean, split and seeds scraped (save the pod for another use)

Crème Chantilly (page 12), for serving (optional)

Tips: I have used Granny Smith apples, as they are firm and hold their shape after cooking. Other cooking apples will also work.

You can also use Pâte Brisée (page 16) as the base for this tarte.

If your puff pastry is frozen, thaw it in the fridge for 2 hours or overnight before using it. Dust your work surface with flour and roll out the puff pastry to a 10-inch (25-cm) square. Use a plate to trace and cut out a 9½-inch (24-cm) circle. Dock the pastry all over with a fork (see page 94). Place it on a baking tray, cover with plastic wrap and chill it in the fridge until you are ready to assemble it, about 30 minutes.

Preheat the oven to 400°F (200°C).

Toss the apples in 1 tablespoon (15 g) of the lemon juice, and set them aside.

In a medium saucepan, over medium-high heat, cook the sugar until it starts to caramelize to a deep amber color, for 4 to 5 minutes. The caramel will start to bubble and become a little smoky; remove the pot from the heat and add the butter all at once. The butter will sizzle and separate, but keep stirring to incorporate it.

Add in the vanilla seeds and remaining lemon juice. Return the pot to the heat and cook for about a minute while whisking. The sauce should come together and no longer be separated. While it is hot, pour it into a 9-inch (23-cm) pie dish.

Arrange the prepared apples in the dish, trying to fit in as many wedges as possible. It may look like a lot of apples, but they will cook down as they bake.

Place the dish on a baking sheet and bake the apples without the pastry for about 15 minutes. This step cooks out some of the apples' excess moisture so the pastry will stay crispy.

Take it out of the oven and let it cool for about 10 minutes. Take the chilled pastry from the fridge and place it on top of the apples, tucking the edge inside the pie dish.

Lower the oven temperature to 375°F (190°C) and bake the pastry for 40 to 45 minutes, until the top is golden brown. Let it cool until warm to the touch, and invert it onto a serving dish. Serve with Crème Chantilly (page 12) or vanilla ice cream, if desired.

   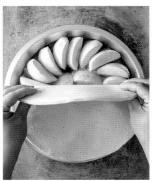

MILLE-FEUILLE

Prep Time: 1½ hours - Makes 6 pastries

Mille-feuille means a "thousand leaves." This pastry consists of three layers of thin, caramelized puff pastry, filled with vanilla pastry cream. It is best eaten right after assembly, before the layers soften. This advanced pastry will take some time to master, and if made properly, the result will amaze you.

½ batch Traditional Pâte Feuilletée (page 95), or 1½ lbs (600 g) frozen puff pastry

½ cup (60 g) powdered sugar, plus more for dusting, divided

2 batches Crème Pâtissière (page 11), in a piping bag fitted with 1-cm round tip

Line two baking trays with parchment paper.

If your puff pastry is frozen, thaw it in the fridge for 2 hours or overnight before using it. If your pastry is in one piece, divide it in half. Roll each one into the size of the baking tray, 12 x 17 inches (30 x 43 cm). It should be about ⅛ inch (3 mm) thick. Let it rest for at least 2 hours, or overnight in the fridge before baking.

Preheat the oven to 400°F (200°C).

Dock the pastry with a fork (see page 94). Place a piece of parchment over the pastry, and stack two more baking trays on top. This is to weigh down the pastry as it bakes so it lies flat. Bake one tray at a time for 15 minutes.

Take out the pastry, and carefully remove the trays and parchment paper from on top. Reduce the oven temperature to 375°F (190°C) and bake for 15 to 20 more minutes, until the top is light golden brown.

Remove the pastry from the oven and carefully flip it over with a large offset spatula, so the flat side is facing up. Dust it with ¼ cup (30 g) of the powdered sugar.

Turn on the oven broiler, and bake it for 1 to 2 more minutes. The powdered sugar will caramelize very quickly, so don't leave the pastry unattended. Take the pastry out of the broiler once the sugar is caramelized to prevent burning. It is okay if some of the sugar is still not fully caramelized; you don't want to risk burning the whole sheet. Repeat this process with the second pastry sheet. Cool the pastry before assembling it.

Trim any uneven edges from the pastry, measure it and cut it into 4¼ x 2½–inch (11 x 6–cm) rectangles. You should get 10 pieces from each sheet, for a total of 20 pieces.

For one mille-feuille, you need 3 rectangles. Pipe the pastry cream onto a rectangle, place another one on top and pipe more pastry cream on that. Dust the top rectangle with powdered sugar, and gently place it on top of the filled pastries. You should have 3 layers of pastries, with 2 layers of cream. Continue with the rest of the pastry and cream.

Assembled pastries are best kept in the fridge and served within 2 hours, as the pastry will become soft once it comes in contact with the pastry cream.

Tips: The biggest challenge to making mille-feuille is baking the puff pastry perfectly. The baked pastry should be caramelized on top, have delicate and tender layers and be golden throughout. The last thing you want is an under-baked pastry where the layers are dense and still soft. The pastry should have structure and be done baking before dusting it with the icing sugar and caramelizing it.

This recipe makes two extra pieces of pastry. Just in case a piece breaks, you'll have replacements.

The start of a biscuit or ladyfinger batter: whip the egg whites until fluffy and incorporate the yolks.

The start of chiffon: egg yolks are first mixed with flour and liquids such as milk and oil.

The eggs and sugar should be whipped to the "ribbon stage" (page 110).

The egg whites are then whipped with sugar until light and fluffy.

Incorporate the flour last.

Finally the egg white and mixtures are folded in together.

⇒ CAKES ⇐

There is an amazing variety of French cakes. Unlike North American–style layered, oil- or butter-based cakes and fillings, French layered cakes are typically made with sponge cake and pastry cream–based fillings. Besides the beautifully layered cakes, many simple cakes, what we know as lava cakes, may also have French roots. Something as simple as a chocolate torte is the perfect dessert.

On the Different Kinds of Sponges

There are many kinds of sponges in the world of French pastry. Most are made without leavening ingredients and are aerated by whipping air into the eggs. Some are made with nut flour instead of wheat flour. This book will touch on a few of the basic varieties.

Génoise sponge: Made using only whole eggs, sugar and flour. The eggs are first whipped with sugar into a foam before the flour is folded in to form a batter. Sometimes butter is also folded in at the end. This is usually a quite dry cake and is soaked with syrup before assembling.

Biscuit or ladyfingers (page 34): The egg whites and yolks are separated, whipped and folded back together at the end. Since the batter is firm, it can be piped into different shapes, like ladyfingers. The result is a light, airy and dry sponge. It is used in Charlotte with Citrus (page 125).

Chiffon: Like the biscuit sponge, the egg whites and yolks are whipped separately. However, chiffon usually has a liquid such as milk or oil added to the batter, then it is lightened with whipped egg whites. The result is a moist, light-textured cake with a tender crumb. Chiffon is used in Fraisier (page 127).

On Whipping Eggs and Sugar

The sponge cakes listed on the previous page all start with whipping the eggs or egg whites with sugar into a foam. When you start this process, make sure your eggs are at room temperature. This will ensure that they will whip to the most volume.

To whip egg whites and sugar (meringue), make sure your bowl and whisk are completely clean and dry. Even the slightest bit of oil or egg yolk in the whites will prevent the whites from whipping to their full volume. Start by turning your mixer on medium; once the whites are foamy, sprinkle the sugar in two or three additions. Adding the sugar all at once will weigh down the egg whites. Once the sugar has dissolved, turn the mixer on high speed and whip the whites to the desired stiffness:

Soft peaks: The tip of the meringue is quite loose, and flops over when the whisk is lifted.

Medium peaks: The tip is firmer, and will hold its shape but will curl over itself when the whisk is lifted. This is the desired texture when making sponges, as it folds nicely into the rest of the ingredients.

Firm peaks: The tip is firm, and can stand straight up when the whisk is lifted.

When whipping whole eggs and sugar, you are looking for "ribbon stage," when the lifted mixture leaves a trail in the bowl for a few seconds that doesn't disappear right away.

You can start with the mixer on high speed, but finish whipping at medium speed, which will create smaller and more stable air pockets in the eggs. This may take 5 to 10 minutes, depending on the amount of mixture. Check for readiness by lifting your whisk and letting the batter flow back down to the bowl, looking for the ribbon. This is especially important because if there isn't enough structure to start with, the batter will deflate when you add flour and other ingredients.

VANILLA ROULADE

This recipe's sponge cake is one reason I started baking at home—it's such a nostalgic dessert for me. A relative gave me the recipe, because she knew I liked to bake occasionally. Without previous experience in making sponge cakes, I was intrigued by the aeration of the eggs and sugar. Whipping the eggs and sugar is the key to a successful sponge cake. Over the years I have made my own adjustments, and the original recipe has evolved into a jellyroll or roulade. The cake is delicious on its own or filled with crème Chantilly.

¾ cup (90 g) all-purpose flour

¼ tsp baking powder

4 eggs, room temperature, separated

½ cup (100 g) granulated sugar

¼ cup (60 g) whole milk, room temperature

¼ cup (56 g) canola oil (or other neutral-tasting oil)

1 tsp vanilla extract

1 tbsp (15 g) liquid honey

1 recipe Crème Chantilly (page 12)

Powdered sugar, for dusting

Preheat the oven to 350°F (180°C).

Line the bottom of a jellyroll pan (10 x 15 x 1 inches [25 x 38 x 2.5 cm]) with parchment paper. If you don't have a jellyroll pan, use a "half sheet" baking tray (18 x 13 inches [46 x 33 cm]). It will yield a narrower roll, and you need to decrease the baking time by 2 to 3 minutes for the thinner cake.

Sift together the flour and baking powder into a small bowl and set it aside.

Beat the egg whites in a stand mixer with the whisk attachment, starting on low speed for a minute; they should be light and fluffy. Add in the yolks, and raise the speed to high and beat for 1 more minute. Sprinkle in the sugar while beating on medium speed and continue whipping for 5 minutes. The eggs and sugar should be at the "ribbon" stage. When you lift up the whisk, the mixture should be so light and fluffy that it leaves a trail on the rest of the mixture while it drips back down. If it is not yet at this stage, whip it for another 1 to 2 minutes.

Meanwhile, stir together the milk, oil, vanilla extract and honey in a small bowl and set it aside.

Remove the bowl from the mixer, sprinkle in the sifted flour and fold it in gently with a spatula, about 10 strokes. Add in the liquids all at once and fold it gently until just combined to prevent too much deflation, about 15 strokes.

Pour the batter into the prepared jellyroll pan.

Bake for 10 to 13 minutes, until the top is light brown. The key to a flexible sponge cake is not to over-bake it. When baking a thin sheet of sponge cake like this, a minute less or more makes a big difference. As it dries out while baking, the cake becomes less flexible. Cool the sponge cake completely before filling it.

(continued)

VANILLA ROULADE (CONTINUED)

Run a knife along the edge of the cake and invert it onto a baking tray. Invert it again onto a piece of clean parchment, so the golden side faces up.

Spread the crème Chantilly evenly on the cake, leaving an inch (2.5 cm) along the top short end. Lift the parchment paper to roll the cake from the bottom short end. Roll as you lift off the paper, trying to roll it as tightly as you can, without pressing out the whipped cream.

Wrap the rolled cake in the parchment and fold in the ends. Transfer the cake into the fridge to chill and set for at least an hour before cutting into it.

To serve, trim the ends, dust it with powdered sugar and slice it to the desired thicknesses. The cake is best served within 2 days. Wrap it in plastic and store it in the refrigerator for up to 3 days.

> *Tip:* There are many kinds of sponge cakes; this one combines a gènoise (whole eggs whipped with sugar and flour added) and biscuit (egg whites and yolks whipped separately and folded back together), with liquids and baking powder added. It is light and airy, yet not dry, which makes it tasty as is or filled. For more on sponge cakes, refer to page 109.

PAIN D'EPICES

Pain d'Epices is a French-style spiced quick bread, loosely translated as gingerbread.
The French version is less heavily spiced and is made with rye flour and honey.
The result is a moist, tender and mild-flavored cake.

½ cup (120 g) whole milk

2 star anise

2 whole cloves

6 green cardamom pods

¾ cup (250 g) dark liquid honey

¼ cup (55 g) unsalted butter, room temperature

1 cup (125 g) whole rye flour

1 cup (125 g) all-purpose flour

1 tbsp + 1 tsp (15 g) baking powder

2 tsp (10 g) salt

½ cup (100 g) granulated sugar

3 large eggs, room temperature

2 tsp (10 g) vanilla extract

2 tsp (4 g) grated fresh ginger

⅛ tsp ground white pepper

½ tsp ground cinnamon

½ tsp ground nutmeg

1 tsp finely grated orange zest

1 tsp finely grated lemon zest

Cinnamon sticks, for garnish (optional)

Lemon slices, for garnish (optional)

Preheat the oven to 350°F (180°C).

Line a 1½-pound loaf pan (10 x 5 x 3 inches [25 x 13 x 8 cm]) with parchment paper.

In a small saucepan, heat the milk, star anise, cloves and cardamom pods over medium heat until the milk simmers, about 2 minutes. Turn off the heat, cover the pot and let the milk steep for 15 minutes.

Turn the heat back on to medium, and add the honey and butter. Heat the mixture until the honey fully dissolves. Strain out the spices and discard them.

In a mixing bowl, whisk together the rye flour, all-purpose flour, baking powder and salt. Pour in the warm milk and honey mixture. Mix on low speed with the paddle attachment for about 30 seconds, until there is no more dryness.

Add in the sugar, eggs, vanilla extract, ginger, spices and zests. Mix on low for another 30 seconds, just until incorporated. Use a rubber spatula to finish mixing in the bowl. Pour the batter into the prepared loaf pan, and place it on a baking sheet.

Bake for 50 to 55 minutes, until the top is golden and a cake tester inserted in the center comes out clean. Let the cake cool in the pan for about 15 minutes before unmolding it and transferring it to a cooling rack. Garnish it with cinnamon sticks and lemon slices, if desired. Store the cake at room temperature, well wrapped, for up to 3 days.

GÂTEAU DE VOYAGE

⇒ Prep Time: 45 minutes - Makes 1 loaf ⇐

Gâteau de voyage loosely translates to "travel cake" and is very similar to a pound cake. This sturdy cake stays fresh for up to a week, is easy to package and could be taken on your journey. Some of the typical flavors are citrus and chocolate-vanilla marble. This recipe has one of my favorite flavor combinations—matcha green tea and chocolate. It can be easily made by hand, or in the mixer.

Matcha Batter

¾ cup (90 g) cake flour

1 tbsp (10 g) matcha powder

1½ tsp (6 g) baking powder

½ tsp fine sea salt

7 tbsp (100 g) unsalted butter, softened

½ cup (100 g) granulated sugar

2 large eggs, room temperature

2 tbsp (30 g) whole milk

Chocolate Batter

¾ cup (90 g) cake flour

1 tbsp (10 g) dark cocoa powder

1½ tsp (6 g) baking powder

½ tsp fine sea salt

7 tbsp (100 g) unsalted butter, softened

½ cup (100 g) granulated sugar

2 large eggs, room temperature

2 tbsp (30 g) whole milk

Tip: When beating the butter and sugar, you are pushing the sugar granules through the soft butter to create air pockets in it. It is important that you incorporate as much air as you can in this step; it is ready when it is pale and fluffy.

The method for making the two batters is exactly the same. I recommend making them separately, rather than making one batch and adding matcha or cocoa powder, to avoid over-mixing the batter and yielding a tough cake.

Preheat the oven to 375°F (190°C). Line a 1½-pound loaf pan (10 x 5 x 3 inches [25 x 13 x 8 cm]) with parchment paper.

Sift the cake flour, matcha or cocoa powder, baking powder and salt into a medium bowl.

In a separate large bowl, beat the butter with a wooden spoon to soften it, add the sugar and beat until light and fluffy, about 2 to 3 minutes. Beat in the eggs one by one, thoroughly incorporating one before adding the next. After adding the second egg, the butter may look a little separated, but this is normal. It is okay as long as there are no big chunks of butter in it.

Fold in the sifted dry ingredients only until there is no more dryness. Last, fold in the milk.

Repeat these steps for the second batter. Make sure your butter and eggs are at room temperature, or they will not emulsify and you will get small bits of butter in the batter. Once you add the dry ingredients, you want to gently fold it in because the gluten in the flour will start to form with the water in the wet ingredients. For a light and fluffy cake, do not over-mix.

Spoon the batters by quarters, alternating between the two flavors, into the prepared pan. Using an offset spatula or a butter knife, gently swirl the batters in the pan. Be careful not to overdo it or the two batters will be mixed and the pattern will not be defined.

Bake the cake for 10 minutes, then lower the temperature to 350°F (180°C). Continue baking for 45 to 50 more minutes, until a cake tester inserted in the center comes out clean. Cool the cake in the pan, then unmold it onto a cooling rack. This cake will keep well tightly wrapped in plastic for up to a week in a cool and dry place.

CHOCOLATE TORTE

→ *Prep Time: 45 minutes - Makes one 8-inch (20-cm) cake* ←

This wheat flour–less chocolate torte is lightened with meringue, giving it a fluffy and light texture. It is made using both dark chocolate and cocoa powder, for an intense chocolate flavor. As the cake is aerated with meringue, make sure it is whipped to the proper volume before incorporating the rest of the ingredients. Made without wheat flour, this cake is a great gluten-free dessert.

¼ cup + 2 tbsp (30 g) almond flour

½ cup + 3 tbsp (60 g) dark cocoa powder, plus more for dusting

½ tsp salt

1 cup (150 g) dark chocolate, chopped, preferably couverture (I used half each of Valrhona's Alpaco and Manjari chocolates)

6½ tbsp (90 g) unsalted butter, room temperature

5 egg yolks

½ cup + 2 tbsp (150 g) granulated sugar, divided

⅓ cup (75 g) whipping cream

1 tsp vanilla extract

1 tsp coffee extract or liqueur

6 large egg whites, room temperature

1 batch Crème Chantilly (page 12) (optional)

Preheat the oven to 325°F (160°C), and line the bottom and the sides of an 8-inch (20-cm) round cake pan with parchment paper.

In a bowl, sift together the almond flour, cocoa powder and salt, and set it aside.

Place the chocolate and butter in a medium heatproof bowl. Heat over a pot of barely simmering water until it is melted, about 2 minutes. Take it off the heat once it is melted—don't overheat it.

Whisk in the egg yolks until they're well blended. Add in the almond flour mixture and mix to incorporate them. Add in half the sugar, whipping cream, vanilla and coffee extracts, and mix until cohesive. Set this aside while you make the meringue.

Beat the egg whites in the mixer with a whisk attachment on high speed for about a minute, until a little foamy. Add in the remaining sugar in two to three additions, and beat until medium peaks form. For tips on making meringue, refer to page 110.

With a rubber spatula, fold a third of the meringue into the chocolate mixture until it's incorporated. Last, gently fold in the rest of the meringue. When you fold the first portion of the meringue into the chocolate mixture, you are lightening the batter, so when you add the rest of the meringue, you will minimize deflating the meringue. Always fold gently to preserve as much aeration as possible.

Pour the batter into the prepared cake pan and use an offset spatula to level the top. Place the cake pan onto a sheet tray.

Bake for 40 to 45 minutes, rotating the pan halfway through. It is done when a cake tester inserted in the center comes out clean. Cool it completely, add a dollop of crème Chantilly and dust it with more cocoa powder before serving. The cake can be served chilled or at room temperature.

Tips: When melting the chocolate and butter, refrain from overheating it as the fat may separate.

Make sure your egg whites are at room temperature so they will whip to the most volume. When making the meringue, it is important that the egg whites are frothy before adding the sugar. If the sugar is added too early when the egg whites are not yet structurally stable, the meringue will not get the most volume.

FONDANT AU CHOCOLAT

Fondant au chocolat, also known as molten chocolate cake, is one of the easiest desserts to make. Be sure not to over-bake these, as you want the center to be deliciously molten and gooey. Served warm, it is so delicious and decadent.

⅔ cup (150 g) unsalted butter, room temperature

1 cup (150 g) dark couverture chocolate, chopped, at least 60 percent cocoa (I used Valrhona Alpaco)

4 large eggs, room temperature

¾ cup (150 g) granulated sugar

½ cup (65 g) all-purpose flour

Butter and cocoa powder, for the baking molds

Powdered sugar, to dust the top

In a double boiler over simmering water, melt the butter and chocolate. Make sure the water is simmering and not boiling. Stir the mixture every few minutes as it melts. Take it off the heat once it becomes cohesive.

In a separate bowl, beat the eggs and sugar until light and fluffy, about 3 minutes. Pour in the warm chocolate mixture and whisk until it's incorporated. Sift the flour, and fold it in with a rubber spatula. Transfer the batter into a clean container and allow it to rest in the refrigerator overnight, or 12 hours.

When ready to bake, preheat the oven to 375°F (190°C). Butter six ½-cup (120-ml) ramekins or baking cups. Dust the insides with cocoa powder (rather than flour), so the cakes don't come out with white spots. Scoop or spoon the rested batter into the molds, and place them on a baking tray.

Bake the cakes for 12 to 15 minutes, until they are cooked around the edges and still soft and runny in the center. Let them cool for about 10 minutes.

While warm, invert them onto a serving plate and dust them with powdered sugar. The cakes are best served warm for the runny center. Cooled cakes can be gently reheated before serving.

Tip: Unmold the cakes while they are still warm; they will come out much cleaner than when cold.

GÂTEAU BASQUE

⇒ Prep Time: 1½ hours - Makes one 8-inch (20-cm) cake ⇐

Gâteau Basque originated in the Basque region of France. It is made with a tender cookie crust and filled with a rich pastry cream. It is like a tart and a cake combined. The first time I had it was at a pastry class. I wasn't sure what it was, asked the instructor, and he told me the name and described it as "quite nice." Consisting of just two components, it is one of my favorite simple desserts, much more than just "quite nice." The tricky part of this recipe is in the assembly—make sure you handle the crust gently.

10 tbsp (140 g) unsalted butter, room temperature

½ vanilla bean, seeds scraped or 1 tsp vanilla extract

½ cup + 1 tbsp (120 g) granulated sugar

¾ cup + 2 tbsp (85 g) almond flour

1 egg yolk + 1 large egg

1 cup (250 g) all-purpose flour

½ tsp salt

1 recipe Crème Pâtissière (page 11)

Egg wash (1 egg yolk whisked with 1 tbsp [15 g] of water and a pinch of salt)

Tip: Work quickly when rolling the dough; it becomes more difficult to handle as it softens. If it gets too soft, chill it in the fridge and roll it again.

In the bowl of a stand mixer, using the paddle attachment on medium speed, blend the butter, vanilla seeds or extract, sugar and almond flour until they're incorporated. Refrain from incorporating too much air. Add the egg yolk and egg, and mix until they're incorporated on medium speed, about 20 seconds.

Add the flour and salt, and mix on low speed for 20 to 30 seconds, just until there is no more dryness. Turn the dough onto a clean work surface and pat into a disk. Wrap it in plastic wrap and let it rest in the fridge for at least 2 hours or preferably overnight.

When you are ready to assemble it, preheat the oven to 350°F (180°C).

Line the bottom of an 8-inch (20-cm) round cake pan with a removable bottom or a springform pan with a piece of parchment paper.

Bring the chilled dough to room temperature until it is soft enough to roll, about 10 minutes. Dust your work surface with flour, and roll out the dough to a 9 x 17–inch (23 x 43–cm) rectangle. Make sure you flour the dough and work surface as needed, and keep turning the dough 90 degrees after each roll.

Trace and cut out two 8-inch (20-cm) circles. Carefully place one circle on the bottom of the lined cake pan. Transfer the other onto a piece of parchment paper and place it in the fridge while you fill the cake.

Gather the dough scraps and roll them into a 24-inch (61-cm) rope. Roll it into a coil and set it around the inside edge of the lined cake pan. Gently press the dough rope onto the sides and bottom edge of the pan. Trim the excess dough.

If your pastry cream is too stiff, mix it in a bowl with a wooden spoon to soften it. Spread the pastry cream onto the prepared cake pan, level and smooth the top. Take out the other dough circle from the fridge, and place it on top of the filled cake. Gently press the edges together to seal in the cream.

Brush the top of the cake with egg wash, and score a crosshatch pattern on it with a fork.

Bake it for 55 to 60 minutes, rotating the pan halfway, until the top is golden brown. The cream in the cake will expand and the surface will crack as it bakes. This is normal and will subside as it cools. Cool it completely before taking it out of the pan. The cake is best served at room temperature and will keep in the fridge for up to 2 days.

CHARLOTTE WITH CITRUS

⇒ *Prep Time: 1½ hours - Makes one 6-inch (15-cm) cake* ⇐

Whenever I make this charlotte, I always make the ladyfingers from scratch. The taste and result are well worth the time! Charlotte is a layered dessert of Bavarian cream, ladyfingers or sponge and fresh fruits of your choice. In the summer, I love making a berry version. If you are pressed for time, you can use packaged ladyfingers, but homemade are recommended.

1 recipe Ladyfingers (page 34), or 40–45 store-bought ladyfingers

Orange Syrup

½ cup (125 g) orange juice (from a medium orange)

1 tsp finely grated orange zest

¼ cup + 2 tbsp (75 g) granulated sugar

¼ cup (60 g) water

Bavarian Cream

1 tsp powdered gelatin

¾ cup + 1 tbsp (200 g) whole milk

½ cup (100 g) granulated sugar, divided

½ vanilla bean, split and seeds scraped (save the pod for another use)

3 large egg yolks

1 tbsp (10 g) cornstarch

2 tsp (4 g) finely grated citrus zest of your choice

1 cup (250 g) whipping cream, cold

Filling and Garnish

1 cup (240 g) segmented citrus fruits (pomelo, orange, lemon, grapefruit), plus more for garnish

To make the ladyfingers, follow the recipe on page 34. You can arrange the ladyfingers into the charlotte's layers or you can pipe and bake two 5-inch (13-cm) rounds for the center and base layers. Bake the disks for 8 to 10 minutes at 400°F (200°C).

To make the orange syrup, combine all the ingredients in a small saucepan over medium heat until it boils, for 2 to 3 minutes. Set it aside to cool.

In a small bowl, whisk together 1 teaspoon powdered gelatin with 5 teaspoons (25 g) of cold water. Set it aside to let it hydrate.

In a small saucepan, heat the milk, half of the sugar and vanilla seeds over medium heat until it starts to simmer. Turn off the heat, cover the pot and let it steep while you prepare the egg portion of the recipe.

In a medium bowl, whisk together the egg yolks, remaining sugar and cornstarch. Slowly pour in the hot milk while whisking the egg mixture. Return the mixture to the pot, and turn the heat back on to medium. Keep whisking the mixture to avoid burning, for about 3 to 4 minutes. The custard will start to thicken, and when it starts to boil, it is ready. Take the pot off the heat.

Whisk the hydrated gelatin into the hot custard to fully incorporate it. Strain the custard into a clean bowl, and stir in the citrus zest.

Last, place a piece of plastic wrap directly onto the surface of the custard, and cool it in the refrigerator until it sets but is still soft, about 20 to 30 minutes. You don't want the custard to be too stiff, which would make it difficult to incorporate the whipped cream.

(continued)

While the custard is setting, whip the cream to soft peaks for 2 to 3 minutes by hand. Keep it in the refrigerator until you are ready to assemble the charlotte.

Whisk the custard to soften it to a creamy texture. If it is too stiff, soften it over a hot water bath. You want it to be soft but not runny. Whisk in one-third of the cream to lighten the mixture, then fold or whisk in the remaining cream.

To assemble the charlotte, lightly brush the bottoms of the two sponge disks and 20 ladyfingers with the syrup. If you're not using the sponge disks, you'll need about 16 to 20 more ladyfingers. Line the bottom and sides of a 6-inch (15-cm) charlotte pan with the ladyfingers.

Pour one-third of the cream into the mold, cover it with ½ cup (120 g) of the diced citrus fruit, place a sponge disk or ladyfingers on top and press down lightly. Pour in more Bavarian cream, leaving about 1 cup (240 g) for the last layer. Distribute another ½ cup (120 g) of fruit on top. Spread the rest of the cream on top, and press the other sponge disk or ladyfingers on top. If necessary, trim the ladyfingers to even out the cake's bottom layer. Cover the top with plastic. Chill it until the cream sets, for at least 3 hours or overnight.

To serve, dip the bottom of the mold in hot water for about 20 seconds, place a plate over the mold and carefully invert the charlotte onto the plate. Garnish the top with more citrus fruit. Slice it to serve.

Tips: Bavarian cream is a combination of custard and whipped cream set with gelatin that provides structure for cakes like charlotte. Diplomat cream is very similar, except it usually doesn't contain gelatin, so it is often used as a pastry filling.

If you don't have a charlotte pan, you can use a 6-inch (15-cm) springform pan, or a cake pan with a removable bottom.

FRAISIER

Fraisier is a classically beautiful French layered cake. Of course, it is the best when strawberries are in season. There are many recipes for fraisier. It is traditionally made with a génoise sponge, fresh strawberries and vanilla mousseline set in a square shape. The cross section of berries around the edge creates its signature look. I used a chiffon cake here instead because I love its texture. This recipe will introduce the rich and creamy mousseline—pastry cream whipped with butter. This advanced recipe may look intimidating, but once you get the hang of it, it is not very complicated.

Chiffon Cake

4 egg yolks

¾ cup + 1 tsp (160 g) granulated sugar, divided

3 tbsp (45 g) whole milk

3 tbsp (45 g) water

3 tbsp (45 g) canola oil

½ cup + 1 tbsp (135 g) cake flour, sifted

½ tsp baking powder

½ tsp salt

5 egg whites, room temperature

Mousseline

2 cups (480 g) whole milk

½ vanilla bean, split and seeds scraped (reserve the pod for another use)

6 egg yolks

¾ cup (150 g) granulated sugar

¼ cup + 2 tsp (45 g) cornstarch

½ tsp salt

1 cup + 1 tbsp (250 g) unsalted butter, softened

To make the chiffon cake, preheat the oven to 350°F (180°C).

Line the bottom of a baking tray (half sheet) with parchment paper.

In a medium bowl, whisk together the egg yolks, ¼ cup + 1 tsp (60 g) sugar, milk, water and the oil. In another bowl, combine the flour, baking powder and salt.

Add the dry ingredients into the yolk mixture, and whisk them into a cohesive batter. Do not over-mix, otherwise the cake will be too dense.

In the bowl of a stand mixer, beat the egg whites on high speed with the whisk attachment for about a minute, until frothy. Slowly sprinkle in the ½ cup (100 g) sugar while beating, and continue beating for about 3 minutes until it forms medium peaks. For tips on making meringue, refer to page 110.

Transfer a third of the egg whites into the yolk mixture and whisk to combine them. Add the rest of the egg whites and gently fold them in with a rubber spatula.

Pour the batter onto the prepared baking tray and level it using a bench knife or offset spatula.

Bake the cake for 18 to 20 minutes, until the top is light golden. When the cake is completely cool, cut out two 8-inch (20-cm) round disks.

To make the mousseline, heat the milk and vanilla bean seeds in a medium saucepan over medium heat until it starts to simmer. Turn off the heat, cover the pot and let it steep while you prepare the egg portion of the recipe.

In a medium bowl, whisk together the egg yolks, sugar, cornstarch and salt. Slowly pour in the steeped milk while whisking the egg mixture. Return the mixture to the pan over medium heat and keep whisking the mixture to avoid burning it on the bottom, about 4 to 5 minutes. The mousseline will start to thicken, and when it starts to boil, it is ready.

(continued)

Simple Syrup

¼ cup (50 g) granulated sugar

¼ cup (60 g) water

1 tbsp (15 g) Grand Marnier liqueur (optional)

Filling

1½ lbs (680 g) fresh strawberries, halved and diced, plus more for decoration

Optional Decoration

Powdered sugar, for rolling

4 oz (227 g) marzipan, colored

Take the pot off the heat and strain the mousseline into a clean bowl. Last, place a piece of plastic wrap directly onto its surface, cool and store it in the fridge for 2 to 3 hours. This can be made up to 3 days in advance.

When you're ready to assemble it, take the pastry cream out of the fridge. In the bowl of a stand mixer, whip it on medium speed with the whisk attachment. The cream shouldn't be too cold when you add the butter.

Add the butter in small chunks, and continue whipping on medium speed for 2 to 3 minutes, until the cream is cohesive. Fill a piping bag fitted with a 1-centimeter round plain tip or snip off the bag's tip to about 1 centimeter wide. Set it aside.

For the syrup, combine the sugar and water in a small saucepan over medium heat and bring it to a boil for 2 to 3 minutes. Add the liqueur, if desired.

To assemble the cake, line the edge of an 8-inch (20-cm) cake ring or a cake pan with a removable bottom with a piece of acetate film or parchment paper. Place a sponge disk on the bottom and brush it lightly with syrup. Arrange the halved strawberries around the edge. Try to use ones about the same size, so they look consistent.

Pipe a layer of mousseline on the sponge and place about ½ cup (90 g) of diced strawberries on top. Pipe more mousseline over the berries and in between the berries around the edge, saving ¾ cup (150 g) of mousseline for a thin layer on the top.

Place the second sponge disk on top, pressing gently to make sure the layer is even, and lightly brush it with syrup. Spread the remaining mousseline on top. Cover it with plastic wrap and let it set in the refrigerator for at least 3 hours, or overnight.

As an optional decoration, dust your work surface and rolling pin with powdered sugar, and roll the marzipan into an 8½-inch (22-cm) circle. Carefully drape the marzipan over the top of the cake and smooth the surface with your fingers.

To serve, transfer the cake to a plate, remove the acetate film or parchment around the sides and decorate it with strawberries on top.

Tips: Though you can make this recipe within 2 to 3 hours, it is much more manageable to split the process into 2 days. Make the sponge and the pastry cream on the first day, and then focus on assembling it the next.

Though optional, the marzipan decoration is classic and gives the cake a beautiful finished look.

To shape small boules, flatten a piece of dough, and bring in the edges.

Cup your hand over the dough and roll in a circular motion.

To shape large boules, bring in the edge of the dough with both hands.

Tuck in the edges with the sides of your hand while moving both hands in a circular motion.

Brioche before proofing.

When perfectly proofed, they should be doubled in size.

YEASTED
PASTRIES

Bread dough can be divided into two categories: lean dough and enriched dough. Lean dough breads are those made with flour, salt and water. Hearth breads are in this category. This book's recipes mostly belong in the enriched dough category— doughs made with the addition of sugar, butter and milk. Tender and rich brioche is an excellent example. Make sure your yeast is still active before using it to ensure the dough will rise.

Proofing

Most bread recipes require proofing (rising) the dough twice so the yeast has time to become active and grow. One way to control and time your baking is to "retard" the dough by placing it in the refrigerator. For example, you can do the first proof, punch down the dough to deflate it, shape it and refrigerate it until the next day. On the next day, you can do the second proof and bake the bread.

The retarding process allows you better control of the baking schedule; it also allows the bread to develop a deeper flavor by slow fermentation. Yeasted dough typically can be retarded for up to 3 to 4 days; longer than that would exhaust the yeast and the dough wouldn't rise. The longer you refrigerate the dough, the less active the yeast becomes. You can tell when the dough is no longer good to bake when you smell a trace of alcohol.

The Perfect Proof

In general, the rule of thumb for proofing is to let the dough rise until it doubles in volume. This is true for the first and second proof, however, the second one is more crucial.

In the first rise, you knock the dough down before shaping it. During the second rise, an under-proofed dough does not have the chance to grow to its full potential, making for a dense crumb and thick crust. If the dough is over-proofed, it will collapse, because it has started to lose its structure.

If you have over-proofed your dough, you can usually deflate it, re-shape it and let it rise again. Of course, you can't repeat this too many times, as the yeast becomes exhausted.

Besides proofing the dough to double its volume, you can also tell if it is ready by gently pressing the dough with your finger. If the indentation bounces back right away, it is not ready. If it comes back slightly and slowly, it is perfectly proofed. If it failed to come back at all, it has been over-proofed.

It is ideal to proof bread between 90° and 100°F (32° and 38°C). Room temperature also works, but it will take longer, depending on the weather. You can speed up the process by turning your oven into a proofing box. Place the dough in the cool oven with a small pot of hot water next to it; check it every 20 minutes. When the dough is almost ready, remove the dough and the water, and preheat your oven to bake the bread.

The suggested proofing times are guidelines; it is much better to observe your dough and its growth. I usually mark down the time when I finish shaping the dough, so I have an idea of how much time has passed during proofing.

Flouring

A common bread-baking mistake is to add too much flour; when we see wet dough, we panic and tend to add more flour. This actually changes the original recipe and will make the bread dry and hard. The gluten in the flour needs time and mixing to form strong bonds, so hold back on adding flour and let the gluten form.

Furthermore, some doughs, such as brioche, are meant to be sticky; it makes a soft and tender bread. Use the same restraint when flouring the work surface; flour only until your dough does not stick.

On Making the Perfect Boules

Many traditional French breads are shaped into boules. Boule is the French term for ball. Before shaping the final product, we often form the dough into a boule before its first rise so it has a nice and smooth surface.

To shape small boules, press down on a piece of dough with your palm and fold the edges into the center to create surface tension. Flip over the dough, cup your hand over it, and using a gentle circular motion, roll it until a smooth ball forms. The bottom of the dough needs a slightly sticky work surface so the ball will form with the circular movement of your hands, so do not flour too much, or it will not stick.

To shape larger boules, use the same technique, but tuck in the dough's edges with the sides of your hand while moving both hands in a circular motion. This technique will apply throughout these bread recipes and with a little practice, you can make perfect boules!

PAIN DE MIE

Prep Time: 45 minutes - Makes one 9 x 4 x 4–inch (23 x 10 x 10–cm) loaf

Pain de mie is baked in a loaf pan with a tight-fitting lid (also known as a Pullman pan), forming its signature square shape when cut into slices. The lidded pan encloses the dough, thereby creating bread with a fine and tight crumb and minimal crust. It is perfect for sandwiches and toast. This is one of the easiest breads to make, even for beginners.

3⅓ cups (500 g) bread flour

1½ tsp (8 g) salt

2 tbsp + 2 tsp (40 g) granulated sugar

2 tsp (6 g) instant yeast

¼ cup (60 g) whole milk, room temperature

1 cup + 2 tsp (260 g) water, room temperature

2 tbsp + 2 tsp (40 g) unsalted butter, softened

In the bowl of a stand mixer, whisk the flour, salt, sugar and yeast.

Mix the milk and water together in a measuring cup and add it to the dry ingredients.

With the dough hook, start the mixer on low speed and mix for 5 minutes, until the dough forms. Add the butter in two additions, mixing for 2 minutes after each. Scrape down the sides of the bowl, and mix on low for 10 more minutes.

Lightly flour a work surface, and grease a medium bowl. Turn the dough onto the work surface, and shape it into a ball with your hands by moving it in a circular motion. Place the dough into the greased bowl, cover it with plastic wrap and let it rise for about an hour, or until it doubles in volume.

Meanwhile, butter the insides and the lid of the Pullman pan.

When the dough has finished its first proof, deflate it and turn it onto a floured work surface. Gently press the dough with your palm, and shape it into a 9 x 8–inch (23 x 20–cm) rectangle. Roll it up from the long side, starting from the bottom. After each roll, gently press down the seams. When you have formed it into a log, pinch to seal the seam.

Place it into the buttered loaf pan, seam down. Shape the log evenly throughout its length to create a loaf with a consistent crumb. Cover it with the lid.

Let the dough proof until it is about an inch (2.5 cm) below the top of the pan, about an hour. When the dough is nearly done with its second proof, preheat the oven to 375°F (190°C).

Place the loaf pan on a baking sheet, and bake it for 40 minutes, rotating the pan halfway through. It is done when the center registers 200°F (93°C).

Take off the lid, let the bread cool in the pan for about 5 minutes, then gently invert the loaf onto a cooling rack and cool it completely before slicing. This is one of the few types of bread that I bake the crust to a light golden color, preserving the minimal crust of the pain de mie.

Tips: You can find a Pullman loaf pan in a specialty kitchen supply store or online.

If the bread expands beyond the top of the pan, simply trim the extra crust after baking.

Yeasted Pastries ⟻ 135

BRIOCHE NANTERRE

⇒ Prep Time: 1 hour · Makes one 10 x 5–inch (25 x 13–cm) loaf ⇐

Brioche comes in all sizes and forms. One of my favorites is brioche Nanterre, where individual dough balls are baked in two rows into a loaf form. You can serve it by tearing the portions, cut into slices to spread with jam or make it into sandwiches. I think of brioche as more like cake than bread, because of the copious amounts of egg and butter that make it incredibly rich and tender. Don't be intimidated by the soft and sticky dough; refrigerate it overnight to firm it up before shaping.

1⅔ cups (250 g) all-purpose flour

1½ tsp (5 g) instant yeast

1¼ tsp (8 g) salt

2 tbsp (30 g) granulated sugar

3 large (150 g) eggs

1 tbsp (15 g) milk

⅔ cup (150 g) unsalted butter, softened

Egg wash (1 egg yolk whisked with 1 tbsp [15 g] of water and a pinch of salt)

In the bowl of a stand mixer, whisk together the flour, yeast, salt and sugar.

Add the eggs and milk to the flour and mix on low with the dough hook for 5 minutes, until the dough comes away from the sides of the bowl.

Add in the softened butter in three additions, mixing thoroughly after each one, about 2 minutes each. After mixing in the last bit of butter, scrape down the sides of the bowl and continue to mix on low for 10 minutes.

In the meantime, grease a medium bowl. Once the mixing is done, scrape the dough into the greased bowl, cover it with plastic wrap and let it rise for 2 to 3 hours, or until doubled in volume.

Knock down the dough, shape it into a ball and return it to the bowl or a container. Cover it and let it rest in the refrigerator overnight. This step is important because the dough is very soft at room temperature. It is much easier to work with after it spends a night in the refrigerator.

On the next day, take the dough from the fridge and transfer it to a lightly floured work surface. Have some flour for dusting handy at your work station.

Divide the dough into 8 equal pieces, each weighing 2.5 ounces (75 g). To shape the pieces, press down with your palm, fold the edges into the center, flip over the dough and cup your hand over it and, using gentle, circular motions, work the dough into a smooth ball. The bottom of the dough needs a slightly sticky surface so the ball will form with the circular movement of your hands; so do not use too much flour or it will not stick. For tips on making boules, refer to page 133.

Butter a 10 x 5–inch (25 x 13–cm) loaf pan, and place the balls inside in 2 rows of 4. Loosely cover the pan with plastic wrap and let it rise for 2 to 3 hours, until the dough has doubled in volume.

When the dough is almost finished rising, preheat the oven to 350°F (180°C).

Brush the loaf with egg wash and bake for 40 to 45 minutes, rotating the pan halfway through, until the top is a rich golden brown color. It is done when the center registers 200°F (93°C). Let it cool in the pan for a few minutes, then transfer it to a cooling rack. Brioche is best served the day it is baked. Store it wrapped in plastic wrap. It also freezes well if wrapped tightly.

BRIOCHE À TÊTE AND BRIOCHE AU SUCRE

⇒ *Prep Time: 1 hour - Makes 12 rolls* ⇐

Brioche à tête was the very first thing that I learned to shape in my first bakery job. Every morning at 3 a.m., I would make the little boules and the brioche Nanterre. I still enjoy shaping them; it feels therapeutic to form dough with my hands. Brioche à tête means brioche with a head, while brioche au sucre means brioche with sugar. The kneading and first proof steps in this recipe are the same as for brioche Nanterre (page 136). Likewise, for both of these rolls, the shaping starts the same; the brioche à tête requires an extra step to create the head.

1²⁄₃ cups (250 g) all-purpose flour

1½ tsp (5 g) instant yeast

1¼ tsp (8 g) salt

2 tbsp (30 g) granulated sugar

3 large (150 g) eggs

1 tbsp (15 g) whole milk

²⁄₃ cup (150 g) unsalted butter, softened

Egg wash (1 egg yolk whisked with 1 tbsp [15 g] of water and a pinch of salt)

Pearl sugar, for brioche au sucre

In the bowl of a stand mixer, whisk together the flour, yeast, salt and sugar.

Add the eggs and milk to the flour and mix on low with the dough hook for 5 minutes, until the dough comes away from the sides of the bowl.

Add in the softened butter in three additions, mixing thoroughly after each one, about 2 minutes each. After mixing in the last bit of butter, scrape down the sides of the bowl and continue to mix on low for 10 minutes.

In the meantime, grease a medium bowl. Once the mixing is done, turn the dough into the prepared bowl. Cover it with plastic wrap and let it proof at room temperature for about an hour, or until the dough doubles in volume.

When it has finished this first proof, knock it down, cover it with plastic and place it in the refrigerator overnight. The dough can be refrigerated for up to 3 days.

On the next day, take out the chilled dough. It will be much firmer than at room temperature. Turn the dough onto a lightly floured work surface and divide it into 12 equal pieces with a bench knife or chef's knife, about 2 ounces (50 g) each.

Shape each portion into a small ball by pressing down with your palm and folding the edges into the center. Flip the dough over, cup your hand over it and, using a gentle, circular motion, work it into a smooth ball. The bottom of the dough needs a slightly sticky work surface so the ball will form with the circular movement of your hands; so do not use too much flour or it will not stick.

For tips on shaping boules, refer to page 133.

(continued)

To make brioche à tête, grease fluted tins with butter. Take a dough ball, and gently squeeze about a third of the dough to make a smaller "head." Place the dough ball on a work surface, and with the edge of your hand, gently roll the dough between the body and the head by sawing back and forth to form a "neck." Pick up the dough by the head, and push the body tightly into the buttered tin. Dip your finger in a little flour, and push it all the way through the dough around the head to tuck it in and form an indentation, about 5 to 6 times. Repeat with the rest of the dough and let them proof a second time.

To make brioche au sucre, place the dough balls on a parchment-lined baking sheet and let them proof a second time.

For the second proofing, loosely place a piece of plastic wrap over the brioche. Let them proof at room temperature for about an hour, or until they double in volume.

When they are almost finished rising, preheat the oven to 375°F (190°C). Brush them with the egg wash, and for the brioche au sucre, sprinkle pearl sugar on top.

Bake for 15 to 20 minutes until they are golden brown. Cool them slightly for about 10 minutes, and transfer them to a cooling rack. These are best served warm and on the day they are baked.

Tips: When egg washing the brioche à tête, try not to let the wash drip down into the tin. As the brioche bakes, the egg wash will bake onto the tin, and it will be difficult to unmold.

If you can't find pearl sugar, you can substitute crushed pieces of sugar cubes.

KUGELHOPF

⇒ *Prep Time: 1 hour - Makes one 8½-inch (22-cm) round bread* ⇐

Kugelhopf is a festive Alsatian bread. Light and yeasted, it is traditionally baked in an earthenware circular bundt mold. There are many versions of this delicious bread; my favorite is studded with plump raisins soaked in kirsch, coated with almonds, soaked in a rum syrup and dressed in sugar. This dough is very much like brioche except with less eggs and sugar, which makes it easier to handle. If you don't have a kugelhopf pan, a bundt pan would work just as well.

Bread

½ cup (120 g) kirsch liqueur

⅔ cup (100 g) golden raisins

2 cups (300 g) all-purpose flour

1 tbsp + ½ tsp (15 g) granulated sugar

1½ tsp (8 g) salt

2¼ tsp (7 g) instant yeast

½ cup + 3 tbsp (170 g) whole milk, room temperature

1 large egg

7 tbsp (100 g) unsalted butter, softened

½ cup (65 g) blanched sliced almonds, divided

In a microwavable cup or bowl, combine the kirsch and raisins. Heat it in the microwave on high for a minute. Set it aside to cool and for the raisins to soak for 30 minutes. Drain off the excess liquid and reserve it for the dough.

In the bowl of a stand mixer, whisk together the flour, sugar, salt and yeast.

In a separate measuring cup or bowl, whisk together the milk, egg and leftover kirsch. Pour the liquids into the flour mixture.

With the dough hook on low speed, mix for 5 minutes, until the dough comes together. Add in the softened butter, and mix for another 5 minutes. Scrape down the sides of the bowl with a scraper or a spatula. Mix it on low speed for 10 more minutes.

Add in the drained raisins and mix for 1 more minute until the raisins are well distributed. Place the dough into a medium greased bowl, cover it with plastic and let it rise for an hour. After the initial proof, place it in the refrigerator overnight.

The next day, generously butter the insides of the kugelhopf pan, and coat it with the sliced almonds, reserving 2 tablespoons (16 g). Set the pan and reserved almonds aside.

Turn the dough onto a lightly floured surface, and form it into a ball. With your thumbs, push the center to form the dough into a ring. Place it on the bottom of the pan. Cover it loosely with plastic and let it rise in a warm place for 2 to 3 hours, until it is doubled in volume.

When the bread has almost risen, preheat the oven to 400°F (200°C). Cover the top of the dough with the reserved almonds, and place the pan on a sheet tray.

Bake for 40 to 45 minutes until it is deep golden brown. The center should read 200°F (93°C) on an instant thermometer.

(continued)

Syrup

½ cup + 2 tbsp (130 g) sugar

½ cup (125 g) water

2 tbsp (30 g) dark rum

Finishing

1 cup (200 g) vanilla sugar (see Tip)

While the bread is baking, make the syrup. Combine the sugar and water in a small saucepan over medium heat for 2 to 3 minutes, until it boils.

When the syrup has cooled, add the rum.

Let the bread cool in the mold for about 15 minutes. Carefully transfer it to a cooling rack. While the bread is still warm, brush on the syrup, at least 4 to 5 coats. It will all soak in. Let the bread cool completely.

Place the vanilla sugar in a large bowl, and coat the exterior of the kugelhopf all over with sugar. The kugelhopf will last up to 2 days at room temperature in an airtight container.

> **Tip:** Use the leftover vanilla bean pod from another recipe to make vanilla sugar. Just place it in your sugar and let the flavor infuse for a week.

TARTE TROPEZIENNE

Tarte Tropezienne is more like a cake, with layers of rich buttery brioche topped with crunchy pearl sugar, and filled with pastry cream or buttercream. The cream is traditionally flavored with orange blossom water, which I have used here. You could use rum or even kirsch if you prefer.

Dough

1⅔ cups (250 g) all-purpose flour

1½ tsp (5 g) instant yeast

1¼ tsp (8 g) salt

2 tbsp (30 g) granulated sugar

3 large (150 g) eggs

1 tbsp (15 g) whole milk

⅔ cup (150 g) unsalted butter, softened

Finishing

Egg wash (1 egg yolk whisked with 1 tbsp [15 g] of water and a pinch of salt)

2 tbsp (30 g) pearl sugar

Filling

1 batch Crème Pâtissière (page 11)

1 tsp orange blossom water

¼ cup (60 g) cold whipping cream

To make the dough, whisk together the flour, yeast, salt and sugar in the bowl of a stand mixer. Add the eggs and milk to the flour and mix on low with the dough hook for 5 minutes, until the dough comes away from the sides of the bowl. Add in the softened butter in three additions, mixing thoroughly after each one, about 2 minutes each. After mixing in the last bit of butter, scrape down the sides of the bowl and continue to mix on low for 10 minutes.

In the meantime, grease a medium bowl. Once the mixing is done, turn the dough into the prepared bowl. Cover it with plastic wrap and let it proof at room temperature for about an hour, or until the dough doubles in volume.

When it has finished the first proof, knock it down, cover it with plastic and place it in the refrigerator overnight. The dough can be refrigerated for up to 3 days. On a lightly floured work surface, shape the brioche dough into a ball, cover it loosely with plastic wrap and let it rest for about 10 minutes. This relaxes the gluten and will minimize shrinking when you roll it out.

Butter a 9-inch (23-cm) round ring or cake pan. You can also make the recipe without one; it will take on whatever shape you roll out. Rolling from the center toward the edges, and rotating after each roll, roll the dough into a 9-inch (23-cm) round disk. Place the disk in the ring or cake pan, if using. Use a toothpick or skewer to dock the dough (see page 94). Loosely cover it with plastic wrap, and let it rise for 1 to 2 hours, or until doubled in volume.

Preheat the oven to 350°F (180°C). When the dough is finished proofing, brush the top with the egg wash and sprinkle evenly with the pearl sugar. Bake for 30 minutes, rotating the pan halfway through, until the top is golden brown. Let it cool completely before filling it.

To make the filling, whisk the pastry cream in a medium bowl to loosen it, and incorporate the orange blossom water. In a separate bowl, beat the cold whipping cream with a whisk vigorously for about a minute, until soft peaks form. Gently fold the pastry cream into the whipping cream. Fill a pastry bag fitted with a 1-centimeter round piping tip with the finished cream.

To assemble the cake, slice the baked brioche in half as for a sandwich. Cut the top into 8 wedges; this way the cake will stay intact when you cut it to serve. Dust the top pieces with powdered sugar. Place the bottom half on a serving plate, and pipe the pastry cream onto it. If you find the cream too loose, chill it for about 15 minutes to firm it up. Replace the top wedges on the filling and dust it with more pearl sugar if necessary. This cake is best filled and served the day it is baked.

BRIOCHE CINNAMON SCROLLS

Once I learned to make brioche, I couldn't make cinnamon rolls with any other dough. Its buttery flavor and tender texture are divine when made into cinnamon rolls. Since the brioche is quite rich, a light cardamom glaze adds the perfect amount of sweetness and spicy brightness.

Cinnamon Spread

½ cup (125 g) unsalted butter, softened

½ cup (85 g) loosely packed brown sugar

2 tsp (10 g) cinnamon

1 tsp vanilla extract

½ tsp salt

Brioche

1⅔ cups (250 g) all-purpose flour

1½ tsp (5 g) instant yeast

1¼ tsp (8 g) salt

2 tbsp (30 g) granulated sugar

3 large (150 g) eggs

1 tbsp (15 g) whole milk

⅔ cup (150 g) unsalted butter, softened

Cardamom Glaze

1 cup (120 g) powdered sugar, sifted

1 tbsp (15 g) butter, melted

1 tsp ground cardamom

2 tbsp (30 g) whole milk

1 tsp vanilla extract

To make the cinnamon spread, combine all the ingredients in a medium bowl using a rubber spatula until it's smooth. Set it aside.

To make the brioche, in the bowl of a stand mixer, whisk the flour, yeast, salt and sugar. Add the eggs and milk to the flour.

Mix on low with the dough hook for 5 minutes, until the dough comes away from the sides of the bowl.

Add the softened butter in three additions, mixing thoroughly after each one, for about 2 minutes each. After mixing in the last bit of butter, scrape down the sides of the bowl and continue to mix on low for 10 minutes.

In the meantime, grease a medium bowl. Once the mixing is done, turn the dough into the prepared bowl. Cover it with plastic wrap and let it proof at room temperature for about an hour, or until the dough doubles in volume.

When it has finished this first proof, knock it down, cover it with plastic and place it in the refrigerator overnight. The dough can be refrigerated for up to 3 days.

To prepare the baking pan, cut a piece of 13-inch (33-cm) round parchment paper. Butter the bottom and sides of an 8-inch (20-cm) round cake pan, and set the parchment onto it.

The next day, take out the chilled dough. It will be much firmer than at room temperature. Turn out the dough onto a lightly floured work surface and roll it into a 12 x 10–inch (30 x 25–cm) rectangle.

Spread the cinnamon spread evenly onto the dough, leaving an inch (2.5 cm) along the top edge. Roll up the dough from the bottom edge and pinch the seam after rolling. Cut it into 8 equal pieces. Place the rolls, cut sides up, into the prepared pan.

To proof, loosely place a piece of plastic wrap over the brioche. Let it proof at room temperature for about an hour, or until it doubles in volume. When it is almost finished rising, preheat the oven to 375°F (190°C).

Bake for 30 to 35 minutes, until golden brown. Cool it slightly for about 10 minutes, and transfer it to a cooling rack.

To make the glaze, whisk all the ingredients in a small bowl. Drizzle it all over the tops of the cooled rolls. These are best served warm and on the day they are baked.

KOUIGN AMANN

⤳ *Prep Time: 1½ hours - Makes 9 pastries* ⬳

Kouign amann (pronounced queen-amahn) originated in the Brittany region of France, and its name roughly translates to "butter cake." This buttery, crispy, flaky and caramelized pastry is so sweetly divine. I think of this as something between croissant and puff pastry with a copious amount of sugar. This advanced recipe requires a technique that folds butter into the pastry. The key to any butter-layered pastry is using good butter and providing time to rest the dough. It is amazing how delicious this pastry is, made from only six ingredients.

Dough

2¾ cups (400 g) bread flour

1½ tsp (5 g) instant yeast

1½ tsp (8 g) salt

1 cup (250 g) cool water

Butter Pack

½ lb (227 g) + ½ tsp per kouign amann unsalted butter, room temperature, plus more to grease the rings or molds, and for the top

1 cup (200 g) granulated sugar

1 tsp salt

In the bowl of a stand mixer, whisk the flour, yeast and salt. Add in the water and mix on low speed with the dough hook for 10 minutes.

Transfer the dough onto a clean surface and shape it into a ball. Place it into a greased bowl, and cover with plastic wrap. Let the dough rise for about 30 minutes, and transfer it to the refrigerator to chill for at least 1 hour or overnight. This dough can be refrigerated for up to 2 days.

Meanwhile, make the butter pack. Fold in the edges of a sheet of parchment paper to make a 6-inch (15-cm) square in the middle. Place the butter inside the square, and fold in the edges of the paper.

Flip the pack over and gently roll it with a rolling pin. The butter should fill in the edges and corners. The goal is to make the butter pack an even thickness and as square as possible.

Place it in the fridge until you are ready to laminate. It is important to get the butter and dough to a similar soft consistency—firm yet malleable.

Take out the butter 10 to 15 minutes prior to laminating the dough. If it is still too hard, roll it again with a rolling pin to soften it. Pastry lamination is repeatedly folding the dough and butter to form a multi-layered pastry. Temperature is key; it is almost always better to laminate with cold dough and butter, but they have to be at the same consistency. For example, if the butter breaks when you roll it with the dough, it won't laminate well because some parts of the pastry will have more butter than others, and it won't bake into distinct layers.

When the dough is risen and still cool, turn it onto a floured surface and roll the dough into a 6 x 12–inch (15 x 30–cm) rectangle. It should be a similar shape and size to the butter pack.

(continued)

Unwrap the butter, place it in the middle of the dough and fold the excess dough from the ends to the center. Pinch the seams and the two open ends.

Turn the dough 90 degrees, starting from the center. Roll the dough into a 6 x 18–inch (15 x 45–cm) rectangle, and fold the dough into thirds, as for a business letter. Turn the dough 90 degrees, and repeat the rolling and folding once. Wrap the dough with plastic wrap and place it in the refrigerator to rest for 30 minutes to relax the gluten bonds, which will make it easier to roll.

Meanwhile, mix the sugar and salt in a medium bowl. Butter nine 3-inch (8-cm) round rings or nine wells of a muffin pan and set it aside.

After resting, dust the work surface and dough with some of the sugar mixture, and again roll the dough into a 6 x 18–inch (15 x 45–cm) rectangle. This time, spread about a quarter of the sugar mixture in the middle third, fold one end of the third to the center, and spread another quarter of the sugar onto the third just folded. Fold the other third to the center, so you have done your last letter fold (a total of three folds or turns). A "turn" is when you have made a letter or book fold with the butter laminated dough. This recipe calls for a total of three turns, each one a letter fold.

Sprinkle more sugar (not all of it) onto the work surface and the top of the dough. Working from the center, roll out the dough into a 13-inch (33-cm) square. The dough will be wet and sticky, which is normal. Work quickly after adding the sugar, or it will turn into syrup.

Trim about ½ inch (13 mm) off each edge, measure out nine 4-inch (10-cm) squares and cut them with a pastry wheel or a chef's knife.

Fold one square's four corners into the center, then gather and fold in the four corners again. Dip it in the remaining sugar to coat the bottoms, and set it in the prepared rings on a parchment-lined baking sheet or in a muffin pan. Finish the rest of the squares and cover them with plastic wrap. If there is leftover sugar, sprinkle it on the top of the pastries.

Let them rise for about 30 minutes until they are slightly puffy. Ideally the rising temperature should be below 86°F (30°C). If it is too warm, the butter will leach out of the pastries.

While the pastries are rising, preheat the oven to 400°F (200°C). Place the rings or muffin pan on top of another baking sheet. This is to prevent the bottom of the pastries from burning quickly. Put about ½ teaspoon of butter on top of each kouign amann. It may sound redundant to add more butter to these before baking them, but as they bake, the butter turns into a gooey pool of liquid sugar in the pastries' center, making them extra moist and delicious.

Bake the pastries for 35 to 45 minutes, rotating the baking sheet halfway through, until the tops are golden brown. I prefer baking kouign amann to a dark color, which gives them a distinct caramelized flavor.

Cool the kouign amann in the pan for 2 to 3 minutes, and while they are still warm, carefully take them out of the pan or rings with tongs and transfer them onto a cooling rack. It is important to unmold them while they're still warm to prevent them from sticking to the rings or muffin wells. Serve warm or at room temperature. They are best served the day they are baked.

Tips: Kouign amanns rise from two leavening actions—first, the yeast produces CO_2, which gives them a bread-like texture. Second, the butter leavens the pastries, creating steam during baking, which gives the pastries a flaky and crispy texture.

You can keep the unbaked pastries in a covered container in the refrigerator or freezer for up to 2 days. When you're ready to bake, let them defrost and rise at room temperature for about 30 minutes, then bake following the recipe instructions.

TWICE-BAKED PASTRIES

Twice-baked pastries are an ingenious way to use up day-old pastries. By adding a few ingredients, stale croissants can become the star of breakfast. For the best results, start with a high-quality pastry such as butter croissants.

On Storing Bread

This chapter uses stale bread like croissants and brioche to make decadent desserts. It might be common sense to many, but freezing your baked bread is actually the best way to store it. But before it goes in the freezer, double or even triple wrap it in plastic wrap to protect it from absorbing odors and from freezer burn. Thaw or reheat the bread in the oven to enjoy. Avoid storing bread in the fridge, because moisture will condense and encourage mold. Storing it in the refrigerator also dries out the bread quickly.

BOSTOCK

Bostock is brioche slices infused with orange blossom syrup and topped with an almond frangipane and crunchy almonds. It is a simple yet decadent pastry. The orange blossom and almond make a surprisingly delicious combination. This recipe also works with tender bread such as a Pain de Mie (page 135).

Orange Syrup

1 cup (200 g) granulated sugar

⅔ cup + 2 tbsp (190 g) water

3 to 4 strips orange peels (optional)

1½ tsp (7 g) orange blossom water

6 (¾-inch [2-cm]) thick slices day-old brioche, such as Brioche Nanterre (page 136)

Topping

1 recipe Almond Frangipane (page 19)

6 tbsp (50 g) sliced almonds (either blanched or unblanched)

Powdered sugar, for dusting

To make the syrup, combine the sugar, water and optional orange peels in a small saucepan and cook it over medium heat until it comes to a boil, about 2 to 3 minutes. Let it cool and add the orange blossom water. Set it aside.

Preheat the oven to 400°F (200°C).

Line a baking tray with parchment.

Quickly dip each slice of brioche in the syrup and place them onto the prepared baking tray. Pipe or spread about 3 tablespoons (60 g) of the frangipane on each slice and sprinkle about 1 tablespoon (8 g) of sliced almonds on top.

Bake them for 20 to 25 minutes, rotating the tray halfway through. They can be served warm or at room temperature on the day they are baked. Dust the tops with powdered sugar before serving.

LEMON POPPY SEED BOSTOCK

I love combining North American classics with French pastries, and bostock is a great way to infuse different flavors. The sweet and cake-like brioche with a nutty and crunchy almond topping is a bite of heaven. I've replaced the orange blossom syrup and almond frangipane with a lemon syrup and poppy seed frangipane, reminiscent of a lemon poppy seed muffin.

Syrup

¾ cup (135 g) granulated sugar

½ cup (125 g) water

3 tbsp + 1 tsp (50 g) freshly squeezed lemon juice

1 tsp finely grated lemon zest

Poppy Seed Frangipane

¾ cup (70 g) almond flour, preferably very fine

¾ cup + 2 tbsp (100 g) powdered sugar

3 tbsp (30 g) poppy seeds (toasted in a 350°F [180°C] oven for 10 minutes, and cooled)

1 tbsp (10 g) cornstarch

½ tsp salt

7 tbsp (100 g) unsalted butter, softened

1 large egg

1 tsp vanilla extract

2 tbsp (30 g) lemon juice

2 tsp (4 g) finely grated lemon zest

6 (¾-inch [2-cm]) thick slices of day-old brioche, such as Brioche Nanterre (page 136)

Topping

6 thinly sliced lemons

Powdered sugar, for dusting

Preheat the oven to 400°F (200°C).

Line a baking sheet with parchment paper.

To make the syrup, combine the sugar and water in a small saucepan over medium heat until it comes to a boil. Turn off the heat and add the lemon juice and zest. Let it cool.

To make the poppy seed frangipane, combine the almond flour, powdered sugar, poppy seeds, cornstarch and salt.

In a large mixing bowl, beat the butter with a rubber spatula until soft, then add in the almond flour mixture and continue mixing until the ingredients are incorporated. Add in the egg, vanilla extract, lemon juice and zest and mix until the frangipane is fluffy.

Transfer the finished frangipane to a clean container or piping bag, and store it in the refrigerator until ready to use. You can make this up to 3 days in advance.

To assemble the bostock, quickly dip the brioche slices in the lemon syrup, letting the excess drip off. Pipe or spread about 3 tablespoons (60 g) of poppy seed frangipane onto the soaked brioche, and top each one with a lemon slice.

Bake them for 20 to 25 minutes, rotating the baking sheet halfway through, until the edges become golden brown. Let them cool and dust them with powdered sugar before serving. They are best enjoyed the day they are baked.

ALMOND CROISSANTS

→ *Prep Time: 45 minutes - Makes 6 croissants* ←

Twice-baked croissants are an ingenious way to turn stale croissants into an even more decadent pastry. The croissants are rehydrated with syrup and then filled with a rich, cake-like almond frangipane. I recommend using the best quality, all-butter croissants you can find. My favorite part of making these is getting to nibble on the crunchy, caramelized frangipane edges on the baking sheet.

6 day-old croissants, sliced in half horizontally (as if for a sandwich)

Syrup

¼ cup + 2 tbsp (135 g) granulated sugar

½ cup (125 g) water

Filling

1 batch Almond Frangipane (page 19), made and ready to use

Garnish

6 tbsp (50 g) sliced almonds (blanched or unblanched)

Powdered sugar, for dusting

Preheat the oven to 400°F (200°C).

Line a baking sheet with parchment paper, and place the croissants on it until you're ready to assemble them.

To make the syrup, in a small saucepan over medium heat, cook the sugar and water until it boils, about 2 to 3 minutes. Set it aside to cool. The syrup can be made and stored in the refrigerator up to 3 days in advance.

To assemble the croissants, brush the syrup onto both cut-sides of the croissant, until the surface is saturated. Pipe or spoon about 2 tablespoons (40 g) of frangipane evenly on the bottom halves. Cover with the top halves. Pipe or spoon about a tablespoon (20 g) of frangipane on the tops, then press a tablespoon (8 g) of sliced almonds into the frangipane.

Bake the croissants for 20 to 25 minutes, rotating the baking sheet halfway through, until the tops are golden. Let them cool, then dust them with powdered sugar, or dust them right before serving. They are best served warm or at room temperature the day they are baked.

Tip: Make the syrup and almond frangipane a day ahead and assemble them the next morning for fresh, warm almond croissants!

PISTACHIO CHERRY CROISSANTS

Elaborating on the classic almond croissant, this twist uses pistachios and sour cherries.
The method is almost exactly the same, with the addition of fruit. Raspberries are also delectable
with pistachios, even better when they are in season.

6 day-old croissants, sliced in half horizontally (as if for a sandwich)

Syrup

¼ cup + 2 tbsp (135 g) granulated sugar

½ cup (125 g) water

Pistachio Frangipane

¾ cup + 2 tbsp (100 g) powdered sugar

1 cup (100 g) raw shelled pistachios (roasted in a 300°F [150°C] oven for 10 minutes)

1 tbsp (10 g) cornstarch

½ tsp salt

7 tbsp (100 g) unsalted butter, room temperature

1 large egg, slightly beaten

1 tsp vanilla extract

2 tsp (10 g) Amaretto liqueur (optional)

Fruit Filling

1 cup (120 g) sour cherries, pitted and halved (frozen or fresh)

3 tbsp (20 g) raw shelled pistachios, roughly chopped

Powdered sugar, to dust the tops

Preheat the oven to 400°F (200°C).

Line a baking sheet with parchment paper, and place the croissants on it until you're ready to assemble them.

To make the syrup, cook the sugar and water in a small saucepan over medium heat until it boils, about 2 to 3 minutes. Set it aside to cool. The syrup can be made and stored in the refrigerator up to 3 days in advance.

To make the frangipane, place the powdered sugar and pistachios in a food processor and process it until the pistachios are quite fine. Transfer the mixture into a medium bowl with the cornstarch and salt.

In a large mixing bowl, beat the butter with a rubber spatula until soft, then add in the nut mixture and continue mixing until the ingredients are incorporated. Add in the egg, vanilla extract and Amaretto (if using) and mix until the frangipane is fluffy.

Transfer the finished frangipane to a clean container or into a piping bag, and store it in the refrigerator until ready to use. You can make this up to 3 days in advance.

To assemble the croissants, brush the syrup onto both cut-sides of the croissants, until the surface is saturated. Pipe or spoon about 2 tablespoons (40 g) of frangipane evenly on the bottom halves. Place cherry halves on the frangipane and cover them with the top halves. Pipe or spoon about a tablespoon (20 g) of frangipane on the tops, then press 2 teaspoons (4 g) of crushed pistachios on top.

Bake the croissants for 20 to 25 minutes, rotating the baking sheet halfway through, until the tops are golden. Cool them before dusting them with powdered sugar, or dust them right before serving. They are best served warm or at room temperature the day they are baked.

> **Tip:** Make the syrup and pistachio frangipane a day ahead and assemble them the next morning for fresh, warm pistachio cherry croissants!

HAM AND GRUYÈRE CROISSANTS

→ Prep Time: 45 minutes - Makes 6 croissants ←

Ever since having a ham and cheese twice-baked croissant in Paris, I have wanted to re-create it at home. The bakery I went to even served it warmed up right away. At most bakeries, ham and cheese are rolled into the croissant. This one had a béchamel sauce, ham and a layer of soft and gooey cheese. It was quite the scrumptious treat.

Béchamel Sauce

2 tbsp (30 g) unsalted butter

2 tbsp (20 g) all-purpose flour

1 cup (240 g) whole milk

¼ tsp salt

¼ tsp ground nutmeg

6 day-old croissants, sliced in half horizontally (as if for a sandwich)

6 thin slices (120 g) ham

2 cups (150 g) shredded Gruyère cheese

Black pepper, to top (optional)

To make the béchamel sauce, melt the butter in a small saucepan over medium heat. Once the butter is melted, whisk in the flour and cook it for 1 to 2 minutes while whisking.

Pour in the milk in three additions, whisking well before the next addition. Adding the milk in small amounts prevents the sauce from becoming lumpy.

Continue whisking the sauce as it comes to a boil, so the bottom doesn't burn. Take it off the heat, and mix in the salt and nutmeg to finish. You can use the sauce right away or store it in a clean container with a piece of plastic wrap directly on its surface to prevent a skin from forming. The sauce can be prepared up to 3 days in advance and stored in the fridge.

When you are ready to assemble the croissants, preheat the oven to 375°F (190°C).

Line a baking tray with parchment paper.

To assemble the croissants, spread about 2 tablespoons (40 g) of béchamel sauce onto the bottom halves. Top each one with a slice of ham and about ¼ cup (19 g) of cheese, while reserving about ½ cup (38 g) for the tops. Place the top halves back on, and sprinkle the remaining cheese on top. Grind a little black pepper to finish, if desired.

Bake the croissants for about 20 minutes, rotating the tray halfway through, until the cheese on the top turns golden. They're done when the cheese inside has melted. The croissants are best served warm or at room temperature. If you wish, reheat them in a 325°F (160°C) oven for 10 minutes prior to serving.

PRALINÉ BRIOCHE BREAD PUDDING

⇒ *Prep Time: 45 minutes - Makes one 9-inch (23-cm) round dish* ⇐

Although bread pudding didn't originate in France, I have used two very French ingredients in this recipe: brioche and praline paste. Bread pudding is an excellent way to use up leftover or day-old brioche. I love the rich buttery flavor the brioche lends to the bread pudding. It is also a great way to use up any leftover praline paste that adds the wonderful aroma of roasted nuts.

1 brioche loaf, about 1 lb (450 g), cut into 1-inch (2.5-cm) cubes, such as Brioche Nanterre (page 136)

1 cup (240 g) whole milk

1 cup (250 g) whipping cream

½ vanilla bean, split and seeds scraped or 1 tsp vanilla extract

3 large eggs + 1 yolk

¾ cup (150 g) granulated sugar

½ tsp salt

¼ cup (80 g) Hazelnut Praliné (page 20)

3 tbsp (20 g) powdered sugar

½ tsp ground cinnamon

½ cup (70 g) whole hazelnuts, toasted and crushed

1 recipe Crème Chantilly (page 12), to serve (optional)

Preheat the oven to 350°F (180°C).

Place the brioche cubes in a 9-inch (23-cm) round baking dish. It may seem like too much, but try to fit in as much as you can. Place the dish on a baking sheet, and bake for 10 minutes. This is to dry out the brioche so it can absorb more custard. Set it aside to cool.

To make the custard, in a measuring cup or clean bowl, whisk together the milk, cream and vanilla seeds. This is to break up the vanilla seeds for better distribution. (If you are using vanilla extract, don't worry about the seeds.)

In a large bowl, combine the milk and cream mixture, eggs, yolk, granulated sugar, salt and praline paste until well combined. Make sure the praline paste is well dissolved in the liquid. If you don't have praline paste, you can omit it or use nut butter with 2 tablespoons (30 g) of granulated sugar added.

Pour the mixture over the toasted brioche. Lightly press down the brioche with your hands so all the bread is well soaked. Let the mixture stand for about 30 minutes.

When the bread has soaked up the liquid, bake it for 40 to 45 minutes, rotating the dish halfway through. It is done when the pudding has puffed up a little, and the custard is set and is no longer liquid.

When you're ready to serve, combine the powdered sugar with ground cinnamon, and dust the top. Sprinkle the crushed hazelnuts on top. The bread pudding is best served warm or at room temperature with a dollop of crème Chantilly.

Tip: You can prepare the custard and bread the night before. Let the bread soak in the custard, place it in the fridge overnight and bake the next day.

NOTES ON ⇒ INGREDIENTS AND ⇐ EQUIPMENT

PASTRY CHEFS LIKE CONTROL

All cooks thrive on control to a certain degree, but pastry cooks are meticulous. We like to control everything we cook: ingredients, temperature, mise en place and presentation in order to bring out the result we strive for. By learning how to control these elements, you too can become a great baker.

MISE EN PLACE

In French, mise en place means "everything in its place." Being organized will make you a better and more efficient baker. In the professional kitchen, cooks have all their ingredients on hand, laid out in an organized way, to streamline their cooking process. This applies to home baking as well. It was almost life-changing when I first practiced this. Having your butter softened, flour measured and sifted and eggs at room temperature before starting saves time and headache!

TIMES AND TEMPERATURES

Patience is a virtue, also a key ingredient in baking. One of the most crucial things I have learned since becoming a professional baker is being patient. When a dough needs to rest or to chill in the fridge, the flavors develop and its gluten bonds relax and become easier to work with. You simply can't speed up this process. If you are in a pinch, make recipes that take less time. If you are going to make a recipe that needs more time, plan ahead and don't attempt to speed through the process. Time will reward your taste buds!

Baking is all about temperatures. The temperature of your ingredients will affect the end result. Most ingredients used in the book are at room temperature, unless otherwise specified.

INGREDIENTS

More so than cooking, I think of baking as a science. Baking recipes are often very particular about the amount and type of ingredients. The first step to successful baking is using the proper ingredients. Many unsuccessful baking attempts happen when we try to substitute ingredients.

A good rule of thumb—use all the ingredients the recipe calls for. Another tip is labeling! At the bakery, we label and date all our ingredients. This habit followed me back home; I like to know what I have on hand and its shelf life.

Butter

French pastries are all about the butter. If you want to take your baking to the next level, I highly recommend using good-quality butter with a fat content of 82 percent or higher, such as a European-style butter. It will give your pastries a better flavor, and often a better texture. Butter is a complex ingredient: it has fat, moisture and flavorful milk solids. It also plays a role in leavening, particularly in puff pastry. All the recipes here use unsalted butter, so you can control the amount of salt that goes into your recipe. Butter can become rancid easily, and can absorb odors, so use fresh when possible.

Eggs

Eggs give pastries their distinct flavor and color. The quality of the eggs you use will be reflected in the taste of the final product. In most cases, it is imperative to bake with eggs at room temperature. Using cold eggs may seize the butter in a recipe. It is especially important in the aeration process because eggs won't whip to the most volume when they're cold. To warm up your eggs, take them out of the refrigerator 30 minutes prior to using them or place them in warm water for about 10 minutes.

Flour

While most recipes in this book use all-purpose flour, if a recipe specifies bread or cake flour, make sure to use what the recipe calls for. Every type of flour performs differently, and we use them to achieve certain results. For example, cake flour is a fine, soft, low-gluten flour that makes cakes fluffy and light, while bread flour is a high-gluten flour that gives bread dough the strength to rise and lends structure to its crumb.

All-purpose flour has gluten content somewhere between cake and bread flours, with slight variations depending on the brand. Some bakers argue that all-purpose flour is good for nothing. However, for home bakers, all-purpose flour is the most widely available. My personal preference is unbleached all-purpose flour, but you can substitute with bleached all-purpose flour; the results should be very similar.

Milk and Cream

Again, use what the recipe calls for. Milk and cream are usually not interchangeable. Their fat and water content are significantly different and will change the pastry's taste, texture and even shelf life. Use them cold unless otherwise specified.

Nuts

Many French pastries contain nuts, most commonly almonds, pistachios and hazelnuts. If a recipe calls for roasted nuts, make sure you roast them until they are brown and fragrant to get the most flavor out of them (the exception is pistachios because you want to preserve their bright green color).

To roast nuts, place them on a parchment-lined baking sheet, and roast them at 325°F (160°C). The length of time depends on the particular nut, and the amount. I roast them for 10 minutes, and then check them every 5 minutes to make sure they don't burn. They are ready when the center is golden and you can smell the fragrance of roasted nuts.

You can get nut flours at some supermarkets and at most health food stores. Store your nuts and nut flours in the refrigerator or freezer to extend their shelf life.

Sugar

Sugar plays many extremely important roles in the chemistry of baking. My mom would often ask me if I could use less sugar in some recipes, and the answer is often "NO." In a simple recipe like a pound cake, the sugar is not only a sweetener, but the action of beating sugar into the butter actually forces air into the butter, thereby leavening the cake batter. Moreover, sugar caramelizes during baking, giving pastries flavor and color. Most recipes here use granulated sugar, unless otherwise specified, such as powdered sugar.

Vanilla Beans

I would say that vanilla extract cannot replace the flavor of vanilla bean seeds. Not only can you see the specks of vanilla seeds, they have a uniquely wonderful aroma. To get the seeds, cut open a bean in half lengthwise and use the back of a knife to scrape out the seeds. Don't throw away the vanilla pods! You can dry them and infuse them in sugar to make vanilla sugar or grind them up to make vanilla powder.

Yeast

The recipes in this book use instant yeast, the easiest type to use. It usually doesn't require dissolving in liquid. I have made bread many times where the dough doesn't rise and it is almost always because the yeast is no longer active.

First, make sure your yeast is fresh and active. To test it, place a teaspoon each of yeast and sugar into a bowl, add a cup (240 g) of warm water and let it sit for about 15 minutes. Watch as it starts to get bubbly and foamy. If the yeast is no longer active, it will show no signs of letting off gas.

Commercially produced yeast has a good shelf life before the package is opened; use it before the "best before" date. However, once you've opened the package, store it in the refrigerator to extend its shelf life. After opening, it should last up to six months refrigerated, but check the package to confirm. A good habit is labeling it with the date opened, as a reminder of how long it's been open. When in doubt, always test the yeast prior to using; that way you are not wasting your time and ingredients.

Since salt kills yeast, refrain from adding salt directly to the yeast when you make your recipes.

EQUIPMENT

Bake with your senses. Precise temperatures and measurements are all important for successful baking, but we tend to forget our senses. Sight, smell and touch can help you sense if your baked good is too light, dark, burnt, soft or firm. If you can tell that you have over-whipped your cream or under-baked your cookies, then you can anticipate what you can do next time to get the perfect result!

Also, having the right equipment will make your baking journey much easier and more enjoyable.

Acetate Film

These firm plastic sheets, thicker than plastic wrap, have a glossy finish and provide support for cream cakes and decorations. You can find it online or at confectionary and art supply stores.

Baking Pans

For sheet pans, I prefer rimmed aluminum baking sheets and parchment paper. In the baking process, you want your baked goods to bake in the shortest amount of time, so you need a baking tray that conducts heat efficiently. Most non-stick coating doesn't conduct heat well, and needs to be cleaned with delicate care. Aluminum is an exceptional heat conductor, doesn't rust and can stand up to scrubbing. The "half sheet" size (13 x 18 inches [33 x 45 cm]) pans will work in a home oven.

Bench Knife and Dough Scrapers

It seems I can never have too many of these; they are like an extension of the baker's hand. A metal bench knife can cut and portion dough, and can easily scrape clean your work surface. A plastic dough scraper with a rounded edge will give you flexibility and a curve to scrape your bowls.

Mixer

I firmly believe that every home baker should invest in a stand mixer. I got my KitchenAid more than ten years ago and it is a workhorse in my kitchen. Make sure to use the correct attachments and scrape down the sides of the bowl as needed to get a proper mix. A hand mixer will work well too, but they are not as powerful and may not work for kneading bread dough.

Mixing Bowls

I use a set of 5 to 6 stainless steel bowls of various sizes. They are perfect for baking because they are light, heat-proof and sturdy.

Oven

The baker's first commandment should be, know thy oven. Since every oven performs differently (convection, size, etc.), your experience will play a big role. Knowing the hot spots and temperature differences will help you determine how to adjust the baking times and temperatures.

I used to bake from an extremely old oven, and it always ran hot, so I had to lower the temperature, otherwise everything would burn! It may also be worthwhile to invest in an oven thermometer to help you along. I bake most things in the middle rack, as it is the most consistent in my oven.

Rolling Pin

Every baker needs a good rolling pin. I like the simplest straight wooden ones. They roll out dough to an even thickness and feel good in the hand.

Scale

The ingredient lists in these recipes are written with both volume and weight. However, measuring in volume is actually a very inaccurate way to measure because ingredients occupy space differently, depending on their temperature, aeration, etc. It is more accurate to measure by weight. I find using metric units is by far the easiest and most straightforward. It also makes scaling a recipe up and down very simple when you don't need to think in fractions. I strongly recommend investing in a digital scale that makes measuring clean and efficient.

Spatulas

Both metal and silicone spatulas are indispensable in baking. I use a set of several small and large silicone spatulas. A set of offset spatulas will also make life much easier for icing cakes and lifting cookies off a baking sheet.

Strainers and Sifters

Sifting and straining are some of the most important small steps to baking. A fine-mesh one will do both sifting and straining.

Thermometer

This is not absolutely necessary, but an instant-read thermometer can help you determine the cooking progress of a baked good such as a brioche loaf or when you are making a caramel. For baking purposes, buy a digital candy thermometer that can measure up to 305°F (150°C).

ACKNOWLEDGMENTS

For years, it has been my dream to write a cookbook, and I couldn't have done it without my teachers and mentors who have guided me through my personal and baking journey.

To Lauren and Will, thank you for finding me and trusting me to write my first cookbook.

To my family, thank you for your endless support and love.

To Jennifer Lam, for the time we spent together baking through the night to keep up with our market demands. Thank you for always being there when I needed you.

To my "Beaucrew," thank you for doing a great job every day, so I could focus on writing.

To JKE, thank you for taking me under your wing and being a great mentor, both in life and in baking.

To all those who left comments on the Yummy Workshop blog, your words of encouragement and support are what kept me blogging.

ABOUT THE AUTHOR

Betty's passion for baking started when she was twelve years old and she set out on a quest to make the perfect sponge cake. Her curiosity eventually expanded into a passion for the art of pastries.

After attending art school, Betty created her blog, Yummy Workshop, to share her love of baking and photography. Trained and working as a graphic designer, she had little formal pastry training. Eventually her passion called and she decided to take on an internship at the French-inspired Beaucoup Bakery & Café, shortly after it opened. There she immersed herself in the world of French pastries, and worked her way up to head pastry chef, along the way earning a scholarship to train at the famed École Gastronomique Bellouet Conseil in Paris. In 2017, Betty assumed ownership of Beaucoup Bakery with her brother, and continues to serve there with quality and care. She lives in Vancouver, British Columbia.

INDEX

INDEX